OLNEY:
ECHOES OF THE PAST

Healan Barrow
Kristine Stevens

D1598900

Published by

FAMILY LINE PUBLICATIONS
Rear 63 East Main Street
Westminster, Maryland 21157

For more titles send or call for a free catalog.

(800) 876-6103

GENEALOGY * LOCAL HISTORY * EARLY MAPS

MARYLAND * PENNSYLVANIA * DELAWARE
WASHINGTON, D.C. * VIRGINIA

Front Cover Photograph: Route 108 just west of the Olney intersection, circa 1940. Photo courtesy of Alvin (Doc) Berlin.

I.S.B.N. 0-940907-27-5

Printed in the United States of America

CONTENTS

Acknowledgements

Many organizations and individuals provided us with information for this history of Olney. The Sandy Spring Museum let us use manuscripts, notes, oral history tapes and photographs that were invaluable. Sylvia Nash, the historical researcher, spent hours answering questions, giving us insight and providing a map of the early land grants. Doris Chickering, museum director, encouraged us and pointed us in the right direction.

Jane Sween of the Montgomery County Historical Society also provided direction, and the files in the society's library were very helpful.

Several long-time residents spent hours telling us about their experiences in Olney as the village changed from a rural farming community to a busy Washington suburb. They told us stories of their parents, grandparents and great grandparents. Stanley Stabler of Brookeville, whose family farmed the Sandy Spring area for generations, explained the farm economy and helped us understand Olney's farming roots.

Several retired doctors told us about the practice of medicine in a rural community. Dr. Richard A. Yates and Dr. Charles Ligon talked about the many changes that took place in their profession.

Alvin Berlin, better known as Doc Berlin, told us many stories about his drug store and its role in Olney history.

Many other people also answered questions and provided information including the late Harry Musgrove of Brookeville; Sam Riggs of Laytonsville; Judy Foshee of Montgomery General Hospital; Lyn Coleman of the Maryland National Capital Park and Planning Commission (MNCPPC) staff; Mike Dwyer, park historian at the MNCPPC; Jim Sorensen, archaeologist for the Montgomery County Parks Department; Ray and Maureen Martin who live in the former Probert/Ickes house; Lon Anderson, former owner of the County Courier newspapers; Scott Robinson, historian at the Sandy Spring Volunteer Fire Department;

Martha Nesbitt, Sandy Spring historian; and Dudley Finneyfrock of Finneyfrock's blacksmith shop. Other residents, too numerous to mention, offered encouragement.

We thank everyone who gave us information that helped us on the road to Olney's past.

Healan Barrow and Kristine Stevens

Chapter 1

A ROAD FROM THE PAST TO THE PRESENT

Olney, home to over 200 shops and businesses and almost 25,000 residents, bears little resemblance to the sleepy rural crossroads village of the 1700s. But a closer look leads down a road where travelers can find bits of history tucked in the most unlikely places -- an 1817 house built for a farmer who patented the first refrigerator; an 1838 homestead used as a private girls boarding school; Civil War bullets and badges hidden in the dirt behind a nearby shopping center.

Olney is the last suburban outpost in upper Montgomery County, Maryland, on Georgia Avenue, north. Located at a crossroads that has always attracted businesses, Olney was originally called Mechanicsville because of the artisans who set up shop around the point where the north-south and east-west horse trails met.

Today the intersection of those two trails, Maryland routes 108 and 97 (Georgia Avenue), still forms the town's commercial core, but the farmers once served by the artisans are gone. Now a sea of houses, townhouses and condominiums radiate in all directions from the commercial intersection. Traffic clogs the roads that were originally carved from hardwood forests to haul farm products to market. Yet hints of woodlands, open space and a few farms remain.

Farming was the primary occupation of the villagers in 1879. Olney's population totaled 75, mostly farmers. Forty dollars purchased an acre of land that yielded wheat, corn and tobacco.

Since farming played such an important role in the lives of the villagers, local farmers organized and built a grange hall on the southeast corner of the intersection in the 1870s. An historian described the grange members as intelligent, enterprising and practical people. The grange provided a place for farmers to meet regularly and share farming and cropping techniques and became the local center for discussing current events and holding social gatherings.

The village artisans -- a blacksmith, wheelwright, carpenter, undertaker, shoemaker, and tailor -- served the farming community. Two dry goods stores dotted the intersection, and a dentist and doctor cared for the villagers. Historians of that period described the church and school as convenient.

Historical accounts indicate the surrounding villages were somewhat more prosperous. Brookeville, two miles to the north, was bursting with a population of 250. In addition to blacksmiths, merchants and carpenters, Brookeville boasted grain mills, a private academy and a public school. Business was described as good and land as highly improved and under thorough cultivation. Brookeville's land value ranged from $15 to $100 an acre.

Laytonsville, six miles west, had a population of 100. That town too was served by blacksmiths, wheelwrights and general stores and its land was valued at $10 to $50 an acre. Both Brookeville and Laytonsville incorporated in the 1800s and, over the years, controlled their growth.

Sandy Spring, a Quaker community three miles to the east, was considered the cultural center of the surrounding villages. The innovative farming techniques and educational philosophy of the Quakers spilled over into nearby communities and greatly influenced Olney's citizens. As early as 1879 four blacksmiths, four carpenters, three merchants and three millers served Sandy Spring residents. In addition "Sandy Springers," as they were called, established a bank and an insurance company and organized a circulating library. Today the headquarters of the insurance company, although much enlarged, is still located in Sandy Spring. A branch of the bank remains in the village, while the headquarters moved to Olney where the surge of growth has been most rampant. The library, too, relocated to Olney to serve the swelling populace.

Washington, D.C., also played a role in Olney's history and influenced its development. Olney farmers hitched horses to wagons, loaded high with hay or vegetables, and followed the roads that led to Washington markets. The capital city was considered such an important destination that by the mid-1800s, one of Brookeville's most prosperous farmers founded a company to build a toll road from Washington to Brookeville. The road, built on old trails, passed through the village of Olney and part of that original route is the modern-day, heavily-traveled Georgia Avenue. These farmers forged a link with the capital city that remains, although today, Olney's chief export to Washington is its residents.

While the Civil War touched the populace of the entire country, the proximity of the nation's capital defined Olney's experience of the tragic event. On September 8 and 9, 1862, Union troops marched out Georgia Avenue and passed through Olney. While the village and the surrounding towns were saved from any real battles during this conflict, both Union and Confederate troops skirmished with each other and the townsfolk as they passed through. Troops defending the cause of both the north and the south raided farms for fresh horses and food and burned acres of fencing for fires to cook their rations.

Olney's closeness to Washington induced prominent politicians and political appointees to visit the village. Newspaper articles indicate that the Olney Inn, located on Georgia Avenue where the Sandy Spring Bank now stands, was the "place to go" in the 1930s, 1940s and 1950s. The inn was considered a gathering place for Washington senators and congressmen and was famous for the mint juleps that were sipped out on the sprawling front lawn. President Franklin Roosevelt and First Lady Eleanor were said to be fond of the fare at the inn. One newspaper account quoted the former maitre d' as saying, "I served Mrs. Truman and Mrs. Eisenhower and knew the Nixon girls when they were quite young."

Washington's nearness to the village enticed some high level politicos to settle in Olney and the surrounding towns. Tucked away in a development behind the Olney Post Office is the farmhouse once occupied by Harold Ickes, Secretary of the Interior under President Roosevelt. In the late 1930s Ickes purchased the 200-acre farm that he called "Headwaters."

Even though Olney farmers and merchants always played active roles in county politics, the town was never incorporated. Montgomery County government provides services for residents, and the County Council makes decisions about the area's growth. Olney is defined as one of 27 planning areas in the county. The area is bounded by Laytonsville to the west, Howard County to the north, Sandy Spring to the east and Aspen Hill to the south. Guidelines for growth are listed in the "Olney Master Plan," which

PHOTO 2   The aerial view of the northwest corner of the Olney intersection (Georgia Avenue and Route 108) shows Alvin (Doc) Berlin's Olney Drug Store, probably in the late 1950s. Until the late 1960s, Olney was considered a rural community. Route 108 to the left and Georgia Avenue to the right were two-lane roads. Photo courtesy of Alvin (Doc) Berlin.

calls for Olney to retain a part of its past rural character, the same character that attracts an ever increasing population to the town. Olney's change from a rural community to a suburban outpost is relatively recent. As late as 1950, farms occupied 67 percent of Montgomery County. During that period Olney continued to demonstrate its farming heritage, and residents from more popu-lated Washington area suburbs recall trips to Olney as "a drive to the country." They remember their taste buds tingled from the best homemade ice cream they could buy at Martin's Dairy Farm, then located just a short journey south from the Olney intersec-tion.

The blacksmith and tinsmith shops of the 1800s occupied the same frame buildings until the late 1970s. Two other 19th century buildings were renovated to serve the slowly growing community -- the grange hall became a grocery store, and an old general store found a new lease on life as a drugstore and soda fountain.

Many Washington area residents discovered Olney's rural flavor when they visited Olney Theatre. Although it was established in the 20th century, the summer stock playhouse adopted Olney's rustic, rural atmosphere. A tree grew through the theater roof and peach baskets surrounded the light bulbs suspended from the ceiling. Up until the third quarter of the 20th century, the picture of rural Olney endured.

As newcomers came to the area, they joined with long-time residents in clinging to Olney's rural roots. But as growth reared its head, some folks talked of building a ring road around the intersection to protect the commercial area. Others felt a ring road would detract from use of a commercial district at the intersection, part of Olney's history.

During this time, the federal government in Washington, D.C., grew. As it expanded, the nation's capital attracted workers who wanted to live in the near-by suburbs. Businesses that contracted with government agencies also settled in the county. Like the growth of any large city, Washington's growth brought pressure on the surrounding areas. The pressure eventually reached upper Montgomery County and forced changes -- the need for increased housing and small businesses in the village.

Today much of the mid-19th century rural flavor and earlier 20th century aura is gone. Where Martin's Dairy Farm once stood, the Silo Inn and Mr. T's Sandwich Factory now stands. When the Georgia Avenue/Route 108 intersection was widened to four lanes in 1978, the two-story frame building that housed the tin shop was razed. The grocery store and drug store, both 19th century buildings, also fell victim to the widening of the road. Rather than artisans and merchants, three shopping centers and several commercial buildings now serve Olney's residents.

Two of the landmarks managed to survive. The old blacksmith shop is still run by the Finneyfrock family, but was replaced by a modern building to house the craftsmen. The Olney Theatre, with its trademark peach basket lights, continues to produce summer plays, but plans are underway to develop year-round productions.

The first subdivisions of Olney that were built in the 1950s and 1960s, Williamsburg Village and Olney Mill, have been joined by townhouse and condominium developments and rows of single family detached homes. Growth will continue, as the master plan indicates additional houses will be built in the northeast quadrant of the Georgia Avenue/Route 108 intersection. In the early 1990s real estate agents refer to Olney as, "a place that appeals to young, affluent couples."

What remains unchanged is the interest of the residents in preserving the town's unique place in Montgomery County. Although Olney is not incorporated, it has a strong business group, the Olney Chamber of Commerce, and an active citizens organization, the Greater Olney Civic Association. These organizations sponsor community events and lobby elected officials when budget and planning decisions threaten the quality of life in the town. Because of strong community involvement, residents enjoy a library and a recreation center.

Even as subdivisions continue to sprout from what was rich farm land where tobacco and grains once grew, Olney has tried to retain its reputation as a rural community. Its growth as a late 20th century town is rooted in the land, and planners occasionally look to history when they want to name streets and facilities. The names of Charley Forest Street and Brooke Grove Elementary School can be traced to the original tracts of land that were granted to early settlers of the 1700s.

Fascinating tidbits about local residents can still be found. They peek out from historic documents -- the farmer who patented the first refrigerator in 1803; a teacher who once taught Robert E. Lee in Alexandria, Va.; area residents who rallied to build one of the county's first hospitals; and the farmers of the Olney Grange Hall who initiated the parcel post service in the U.S. postal system.

A trip through Olney's history travels a road from the past to the present and uncovers the invaluable treasures this once sleepy crossroads village still holds.

Chapter 2

LAND SPECULATORS, EARLY SETTLERS
AND VILLAGE GHOSTS

Investing in land to make a profit has always been a popular business venture, and often, a significant source of family wealth. Land speculators have been in business in Olney for over 250 years -- long before the county had its current name, or for that matter, Olney even reached the status of a village. Much like the real estate brokers of today, the early land speculators needed ready cash and influence to turn this natural resource -- land -- into a profit-making enterprise.

THE BEGINNING

Land as a commodity in Maryland, dates back to 1632 when King Charles I of England granted a charter to one of the influential members of his court, Sir George Calvert, the First Lord of Baltimore. Calvert, who was given land north of the existing Virginia colony, named his grant Maryland after Queen Henrietta Maria. The charter gave Lord Baltimore and his heirs the right to grant land to settlers and to make laws with the consent of the freemen.

As Maryland's founder, Calvert was no stranger to the hardships of establishing a colony. Before he requested the Maryland charter, Calvert had set up a colony in Newfoundland, but the cold, inhospitable climate eventually forced him to abandon the territory. All along Calvert had kept his eye on Virginia's progress, especially while serving on the council that monitored Virginia affairs after it became a crown colony. However some of Virginia's colonizers were not happy that Calvert managed to get the land just north of them.

From the beginning, George Calvert planned for the Maryland colony to be a profit-making venture. But he never reaped the rewards of his new Maryland colony because he died before King

Charles signed the charter. George's son Cecil Calvert, second Lord Baltimore, followed through on his father's plan.

The early Maryland colonists received land as a bonus for settlement in the new province but had to pay an annual fee or tax known as a "quitrent" to Lord Baltimore. The fee provided a personal income for the lord proprietor. In return the colonists owned the land, could rent or sell it, or maintain it and leave the property to heirs.

Over time the Calverts developed a system of charging for the land and asked for "caution" or "purchase" money. First, a land speculator purchased a warrant or a guarantee for an amount of acreage. The warrant was purchased with money or tobacco, the main source of currency. The land speculator then had two choices. He could file for the deed to the property or hold onto the warrant.

If the land speculator chose to file for the deed, the land had to be surveyed and certain information had to be provided to the land office. After receiving the deed, the new owner had to pay the quitrent or tax.

Some land speculators wanted to avoid paying the annual quitrent. To escape the tax the speculator could hold the warrant and evade the land survey. However this option kept the contiguous land from being patented. Without a survey, no one was certain where the boundaries of one parcel began and ended.

Speculators who were interested in an immediate profit might survey and patent the land grant and lease it to tenants. The tenants were required to clear and improve the land and pay rent with some of their harvest. When the lease ended, the land owner had a developed piece of property and a return on his investment. Or, speculators might divide part of the land into smaller farms and sell each of them, thereby raising the money to pay the quitrent on the entire property.

While some speculators bought land as an investment, others purchased property for themselves or their children. But whatever the reason for the land purchase, the would-be purchasers had the same characteristics -- well-to-do men who had influence in the lord proprietor's government. The Olney area had both kinds of land speculators -- absentee landlords and well-to-do settlers.

OLNEY'S FIRST LAND SPECULATOR

Major John Bradford was the first land speculator to recognize the Olney area's investment potential. As a Prince George's County tobacco merchant he possessed the money, the knowledge and the influence to invest in land to make a profit. He also understood the land grant system and used his knowledge to acquire land.

In addition Bradford had joined a group of Rangers who patrolled the area for marauding Indians and runaway indentured servants. Historic documents suggest that American Indians did not settle in this region. But settlers feared the Indians who came through from the north to hunt, fish or trade with other tribes to the south. In 1694 the Maryland legislative body formally established the rangers to patrol certain areas and protect the early settlements from the Indians.

Bradford probably discovered the fertile land of the Olney area through his job. Imagine what he saw when he came to the Olney area -- forests of maple, hickory, oak and poplar, sparkling streams, wild deer, black bear and bobcats. Bradford rode through these forests on trails the Indians had cleared by burning the underbrush.

Aside from any land investment benefits Bradford derived by serving as a ranger, he enjoyed another advantage. His friend, Daniel Dulany, was a member of Lord Baltimore's government. Dulany held numerous offices in the provincial government and invested in a number of land speculation ventures. One of these ventures involved Bradford, and the two men worked together to seek out the best land in the Potomac valley. When Bradford saw a piece of land he liked, he asked Dulany to make application for a warrant, the first step in getting a patent or grant of the land.

After claiming the land with warrants, Bradford chose to have his parcels surveyed. As an investor seeking a return on his money, Bradford wanted the best land. During the survey it is likely that he rode horseback over the property, picking and choosing the finest sites. Often the starting point for a survey was a tree. If he recognized a rocky terrain, Bradford might leave out that portion. On the other hand, if he noticed a particular plot with rich soil, the area was likely to be included. Other land speculators did the same. When transferred to paper the survey often ended up as curved and zigzagged lines. The result was parcels of property that looked like the pieces of a jigsaw-puzzle.

Today historical researchers who read the old surveys have a difficult time fitting the many irregular land grant pieces together in an accurate map of the properties. Old markers like trees, rocks or posts have disappeared, and the maps and survey methods of the 1700s were not nearly as exacting as they are today. Although the land grants appear to fit together in the illustration of the Olney-area patents, in reality several of the pieces don't quite adjoin each other and some even overlap.

Bradford's first land purchase in the region was 2,658 acres, bought in 1713. Since land grants had to be named before they could be recorded, he called his parcel "Bradford's Rest." A few years later Bradford acquired additional property contiguous to the original land which enlarged his holdings to over 4,900 acres. That property included present-day Muncaster Mill Road, Lake Needwood Park and Brooke Manor Country Club.

Bradford continued acquiring land in what was to become Olney. In 1719 he patented "Charley Forest," a tract of 1,230 acres that included the present-day Montgomery General Hospital as well as the Olney Village Mart. He divided a portion of the tract into four small farms and sold them to settlers who lacked the influence that was typically needed to acquire grants in their own names.

Much like a real estate investor of today, Bradford used the money to pay the quitrent on the entire property.

Other speculators also joined in the drive to invest in the colony's most precious resource -- land. One of the most influential absentee landlords was Richard Snowden. Although most of his large land grants, like "Snowden's Manor" were in the Sandy Spring and Spencerville area, he and his family left a mark on Olney too.

Snowden, a member of the Society of Friends known as Quakers, had an ironworks in Laurel. He probably saw the hardwood forests of his land grants as a source of fuel for smelting iron. He also encouraged his children to consider this area as a place to live.

MAP OF OLNEY AREA LAND GRANTS

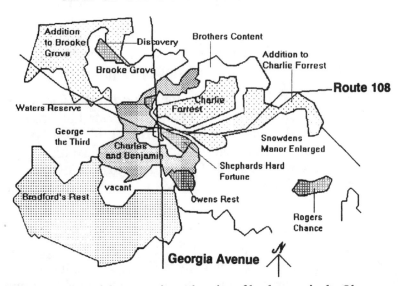

Figure 1. A map of the approximate location of land grants in the Olney area. Map and land grant information provided by courtesy of Sylvia Nash, historical researcher at the Sandy Spring museum.

EARLY SETTLEMENT

James Brooke, a ward of Snowden's, took the advice seriously. Brooke had married Snowden's daughter Deborah. Heeding his father-in-laws's recommendation, he sold the land he had inherited from his father in lower Prince George's County and purchased property in this region. In 1728 Brooke bought "Charley Forest" from Bradford.

Brooke built a frame house with hand-hewn siding north of today's Sandy Spring Post Office in the Brooke Road area. He became one of the first settlers in this region, and his house stood until the early 1900s when it was demolished.

Like Bradford, Brooke probably caught the excitement of land speculation. In 1728 he received a grant for "Brooke Grove," a tract that was located on the north side of Route 108. The tract included Falling Green, one of the few old houses still standing, and continued north on Georgia Avenue to Longwood Recreation Center. Brooke also acquired tracts of land that were contiguous to "Brooke Grove," naming them "Addition to Brooke Grove," and purchased the four farms that Bradford had sold from the original "Charley Forest" tract.

The most interesting mystery in the local land grant story is the shape of the parcel called "Brother's Content." Since the parcel completely surrounds the "Charley Forest" grant, an historian sometimes refers to "Brother's Content" as "a noose around Charley Forest." No one knows why the parcel was surveyed in the noose-like shape, but Brooke did purchase it, thus breaking out of the "noose." By 1763 Brooke had acquired over 22,000 acres, and was considered one of the largest landowners in what later would become Montgomery County.

As one of the earliest families to settle in the region, the Brookes did not remain neighborless at their new home at "Charley Forest." Deborah's two sisters and their families also heeded the advice of Richard Snowden and settled on part of "Snowden Manor," their father's property. All three families were members of the Society of Friends, and these early settlers helped found the village of Sandy Spring, the Quaker community that influenced Olney's early development.

James and Deborah Brooke had six children and gave each of them land to build homes in the area. In the late 1750s Roger IV built a house named Brooke Grove off the road that is today called Brooke Grove Road. His grandson built a new house on that site in 1860, and the building is now part of the Brooke Grove Nursing Home. In 1764 Basil received land between Olney and Laytonsville and built a brick home named Falling Green that is still standing just west of the Olney Mill community.

REVOLUTIONARY WAR PATRIOT AND GHOST

As a town, Olney owes its roots and its first account of a village ghost to Brooke's son, Richard. Around 1760 Richard settled on a portion of his father's land in the area that is today the Olney Village Mart. Richard built Fair Hill, a charming two-story frame and brick building, and the beautiful house stood until the late 1970s when it was destroyed by fire.

The property line of the Fair Hill farm was east of today's Georgia Avenue/Route 108 intersection. But adjacent to Richard's land was a tiny parcel of about 40 acres that had never been claimed. In 1763 Richard bought the parcel from Frederick Calvert, then Lord Baltimore, and named it "George The Third." Today the 40-acre parcel is the northwest and northeast quadrants of the Georgia Avenue/Route 108 intersection -- part of the commercial hub of Olney today.

Besides managing his farm, Richard played an active role in Maryland politics. Like many farmers trying to make a living he must have been angry when the British levied unreasonable taxes on the colonies. In 1774 he learned that the British Parliament was punishing Boston with numerous restrictions because of the Boston Tea Party. Richard and fellow Quaker Evan Thomas joined other landowners in a meeting at Hungerford Tavern in what is now Rockville. They signed a resolution, the Hungerford Resolves, to support Boston and boycott British commerce until Parliament lifted the blockade of Boston's harbor and repealed the tax laws.

Richard continued active opposition to British oppression. In June 1774 he went to Annapolis for the first Maryland Convention where a decision was made to boycott British imports.

Since the Quakers believed in a policy of non-violence, Richard, Evan Thomas and other Quakers must have often discussed the news of the day. Richard became a delegate to the second Maryland Convention, but Thomas dropped out of the proceedings because he did not like the talk of war. Thomas' fears were justified. The convention voted to form a militia.

At the Maryland Convention in 1775, Richard signed the Association of the Freemen of Maryland. The document called for the use of force in opposing the British army.

Records of Richard's military service pose more questions than answers. According to information from the *Calendar of Maryland State Papers--The Red Books* in the Maryland State Archives, Richard received a commission as a first major of the 29th Battalion of the Frederick County Militia on January 3, 1776. But on August 15, 1776 he resigned his commission. The resignation letter, preserved in the State Archives, stated: "Finding my enemies have been so far successful in poisoning the minds of the 29th battalion of militia that a majority are against my acting as major, I therefore take the liberty of enclosing my commission. I would not have it understood by this resignation that I have deserted the common cause. No sir, I will most cheerfully when necessary, hazard my life and fortune in defence of the Rights and Liberties of America..."

About a year later Richard decided, once again, to join the Revolutionary forces. In a letter to Maryland Governor Thomas Johnson dated August 23, 1777 in the State Archives Richard wrote: "...I am again preparing to turn out. I flatter myself I can perform the duty of brigade major tollarby well..."

Brooke probably served as a major under General William Smallwood who participated in George Washington's October 4, 1777, attack on Germantown, just north of Philadelphia. There is an intriguing letter about the battle written to Maryland Governor Thomas Johnson and dated October 10, 1777, that is preserved in the State Archives. The letter was written from a camp near Philadelphia and refers to a Major Brooke who carried the letter to the governor.

Brooke was then commissioned as a colonel under General Smallwood but did not deep the appointment long. In another letter in the State Archives that was written by Brooke to the governor and dated October 15, 1777, Brooke resigned his recent appointment as a colonel. In the letter Brooke wrote that he resigned because of "bad health, brought on by the fatigue of battle."

Brooke's service did not end with his resignation. Sometime later, presumably after he recovered, he began collecting wheat in Montgomery County for the military. Historians note that Maryland provided supplies for the Continental Army. In the "Journal and Correspondence of the Council of Safety" there is a notation that on April 16, 1779, Colonel Rawlings was authorized to pay Richard Brooke 2,000 pounds for buying wheat and flour for the army.

Records of Richard Brooke's military service tend to be confusing because of the way he signed his first name. Like many men of his day, Richard did not have a middle name. He abbreviated his first name and included a period when he signed his correspondence -- Richd. Brooke. He wrote the "d" with a flair and occasionally a modern-day researcher misreads the "d" as a middle initial.

Despite the confusing records, it is evident that Brooke was committed to the colonies' freedom from Britain. But his service in the militia conflicted with the non-violence policy of the Quaker community. Local histories often note that the war affected his health. Brooke died in 1788 at the age of 52, and was buried at his Fair Hill homestead near the barn. But his story does not end there. According to local tradition Brooke's war service condemned his spirit to ride a horse up and down the stairs of his Fair Hill house at midnight.

Brooke's story continues into the present century. In 1932 the Janet Montgomery Chapter of the Daughters of the American Revolution (D.A.R.) marked the major's burial site with a stone marker. A photograph of the ceremony shows the stone surrounded by corn stubble. For many years local residents visited and cared for the site, but during World War II the stone marker was mysteriously removed. Since the grave was no longer marked, its exact location was forgotten. The Olney Village Mart shopping center was built on the Fair Hill farm in 1978, adding to the confusion of the grave's site.

In 1992 an anonymous caller informed the D.A.R. and the Sandy Spring Museum that Brooke's stone marker was at a private residence north of Baltimore. The stone marker was returned to the museum, where it now lies. Today it is difficult to determine the exact location of the actual grave although it is believed to be somewhere under the parking lot of the shopping center.

A SECOND GHOST

When Richard Brooke died, he left his estate to his only child, Ann. In 1802 after she died, the house and parcels of the land changed hands several times. In 1803 George Ellicott of Baltimore purchased Fair Hill and leased it to Whitson Canby who ran a pottery in Olney. Canby needed the house for the eight Irish families that worked in his pottery factory. According to tradition one of the Irish potters hanged himself in the cellar. From then on, the story is told, Brooke had help with haunting Fair Hill.

BIRTH OF MONTGOMERY COUNTY

Until the mid-1770s Brooke and other influential landowners were residents of what was then a portion of Frederick County. In 1776 the Maryland Constitutional Convention divided Frederick County into three smaller sections. One section remained Frederick County. One of the two new counties that was formed was named in honor of General Richard Montgomery who served with the British Colonial Army that fought against the French from 1754-1763. During the Revolutionary War, Montgomery was a brigadier general for the American army, and died in battle in 1775. Although there are many counties named in his honor across the country, Montgomery County, Maryland, is believed to have been the first to have shown tribute to this great American patriot.

Shortly after Montgomery County was established, the area was divided into tax districts. "Upper Newfoundland Hundred" was the name given for the area that today comprises Olney, Brookeville, Sandy Spring and Laytonsville. According to Jane Sween in *Montgomery County: Two Centuries of Change* (1984), the term "Hundred" came from feudal England and described an area where 100 men would support the local lord in an armed conflict.

In 1798 election districts were created, making it more convenient for citizens because they no longer needed to go to the courthouse to vote. Five districts were established and Olney became part of the fourth which was named "Berry's District." The name refers to a storehouse where citizens voted, and the storehouse was named because of its location near Richard Berry's farm. In 1878 the county was redivided into eight election districts. Mechanicsville or Olney was located in the Mechanicsville district.

Montgomery County's land value has always been influenced by its proximity to its next-door neighbor, the nation's capital. During the American Revolution, Georgetown became a major port for shipping military supplies. In the 1790s when President

Washington was looking for a site for the new capital city, several states recognized the advantages of having it in their backyards. Pennsylvania touted Philadelphia; New Jersey lauded the virtues of Trenton; and Maryland agreed to give up its Georgetown port for the new federal city. When the land adjacent to Georgetown was selected for the site, land values in the county increased, as they did once again following the Civil War.

Today the nation's capital still influences the land values in the county. Even though Olney is one of the last suburban outposts on Georgia Avenue north, residents who move into the Washington Metropolitan Region quickly recognize the high cost and inflated value of real estate when compared to similar towns in other areas of the country.

Although agriculture will always be a part of Montgomery County, the focus of land use seems to have changed -- from agricultural to suburban. But the most basic reason for buying and developing land remains the same as it did centuries ago -- a profit-making enterprise that began in the early 1700s.

Chapter 3

A DINGY OLD PLACE

In 1926 Charles F. Brooke (1850-1940) wrote a paper describing the Olney of the 1800s as "a dingy old place" where "little was done in the way of civic improvement." The village, from its beginning, was a junction of two narrow dirt roads that led to other places -- west to Frederick, east to Ellicott City and Baltimore, north to Westminster and south to Georgetown and Washington, D.C. Since the crossroads attracted artisans, Mechanicsville became the town's first name.

Picture the crossroads as Whitson Canby (c. 1751-1823), one of the first artisans, must have seen it in about 1806 -- rutted, unpaved ox-cart trails near a two-story farmhouse called Fair Hill, a smattering of log cabins and acres of land that was ripe for farming. As a Quaker from Pennsylvania, Canby may have been attracted to the area because of the growing number of Quakers who settled nearby. Or perhaps he noticed that one of the ox-cart trails led to potential markets in nearby Georgetown and Washington, D.C.

PHOTO 3 The Olney House as it looked in 1975. Today the house is used by businesses. Photo courtesy of the Park Historian's Office, Maryland-National Capital Park and Planning Commission.

According to tradition Canby bought a one-acre parcel of the Fair Hill property and established a pottery on what is today the northeast quadrant of the Georgia Avenue/Route 108 intersection. He boarded the families of his eight Irish pottery workers at the adjacent Fair Hill farmhouse. Canby purchased land across the street for his own house, known as the Olney House. Although the Olney House has undergone extensive additions and renovations, Canby is said to have built the core of the house -- the kitchen and central part.

Like merchants today, Canby advertised for customers. In 1818 he placed an ad in the Daily National Intelligencer, a Washington, D.C., newspaper. The style of the ad is quite different from the ads of today. The notice read: "Earthern Ware by wholesale. The subscriber, near the General Post Office, informs those persons who deal in the article of Earthern Ware that he has on hand an assortment and intends keeping a constant and general supply, from the Fair Hill manufactory in Montgomery County, which will be sold here at the factory wholesale prices. Those who wish to purchase, are requested to call and examine for themselves."

Around 1826 Richard Butt took over the pottery. He, too, advertised in a local newspaper, but his ad seemed more cordial. He told the public that he was "ready to serve customers."

Today little is known about the pottery factory except that it was the only factory of its kind in Montgomery County. Historians believe that Canby made utilitarian ware like jugs, bowls, mugs and chamber pots. Finer pieces, like teapots that were fired at higher temperatures, were known to be available from well-known factories in Alexandria, Virginia.

Unfortunately no samples of Canby's earthern ware pottery have survived. However in 1980 a local archeologist unearthed a lead-glazed milk bowl near an historic house outside of Laytonsville. Although no markings indicate where the bowl was made, it is believed that the pottery may have come from the Fair Hill factory. The iron-flecked clay from which the bowl was made is native to this area, and the archeologist said it was likely that residents would have bought their everyday earthern ware at the Fair Hill manufactory.

Another clue suggested the bowl may have come from the Olney pottery. A wine bottle seal, with the initials W.C., was discovered at the same dig. In the early 1800s sealed wine bottles were exchanged among the gentry. The initials "W.C." could have stood for Whitson Canby.

In addition there is an intriguing reference on the G.M. Hopkins 1879 map about a small place called Claysville that was located between Laytonsville and Olney on today's Route 108. Tradition says the site was named for the good clay that was in the area. No one knows if the spot was the source of clay for the pottery.

Canby was not the only businessman at the crossroads. J. Thomas Scharf, in the *History of Western Maryland 1882,* lists Benedict Duley as opening the first store and William Starkey as "keeping" the tavern. William Kelly, who also came from Pennsylvania, set up a blacksmith and wheelwright shop.

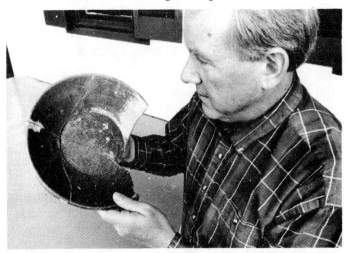

PHOTO 4 Jim Sorensen, archaeologist for the Montgomery County Department of Parks, holds a milk bowl that may have been made at Canby's pottery. Photo courtesy of Mark D. Faram.

In 1806 Kelly hired his 17-year-old brother-in-law, Moses Barnsley, to help in the business. Moses capitalized on his opportunity. He eventually became owner of the business and used some of his profits to acquire farm land.

In his paper Charles F. Brooke also said the blacksmith shop was constructed of logs and capped with a high-pitched roof. Like most blacksmith shops the inside was dirty, smelly and noisy. The forge or furnace for heating the iron dominated the shop. Bellows provided blasts of air to fan the fire to heat the iron so it could be shaped. Years of experience and skill were required to judge the temperature of the fire by its color and to regulate the heat.

Farmers and fellow artisans kept the smithy busy. Customers came for nails, hoes, axes, scythes, andirons, cooking kettles and most any iron object they needed. The blacksmith also shod horses and oxen.

Brooke said there was a free-black helper in the shop "...named Washington Hodge, whom I thought a giant, because of his size and great strength. In one corner of the shop were the stocks in which oxen were placed to shoe them. There are some...who may not know that they were often shod like horses, with the difference that the shoes were in two pieces, to suit their cloven feet."

Moses Barnsley's sons, William, James and John, continued the blacksmith and wheelwright business and gained their own fame as gifted artisans. As wheelwrights William and John made wagons and coffins, served as undertakers and built grain cradles. Local lore has it that the brothers were well-known for their grain cradles, a hand tool with fork-like prongs and a scythe attached to a handle. Farmers used the tool to cut the wheat that fell onto the prongs then dumped the wheat onto the ground in a small bundle before cutting the next swath of wheat.

The Barnsleys, like Canby, had homes in the village. By 1820 the Quakers had bought Fair Hill and established a boarding school. About 10 years later there were enough businesses and residents for Mechanicsville to have its own post office.

From 1829 to 1837 Mechanicsville had three postmasters, and all were teachers at Fair Hill Boarding School according to U.S. Postal records. They were compensated by collecting money for a letter that was received. The amount charged for each letter depended upon how far it had traveled and how many sheets were in the envelope. Based upon this system, the annual salaries of the three postmasters ranged from $7.11 to $22.63.

The local postal system had a short life. Postal records make no mention of the Mechanicsville post office after 1837. By the time the residents asked for another post office in 1851, the postal system said the town's name had to be changed because there was already a Mechanicsville Post Office in southern Maryland. How the name "Olney" was chosen remains uncertain. However it seems reasonable to assume that residents picked the name of the Olney house. Houses had names in the 19th century to prevent confusion since several generations of the same family often lived within miles of each other.

Although Whitson Canby had built the house, a subsequent owner, who loved poetry, named it Olney. Dr. Charles Farquhar had moved to Mechanicsville from Alexandria in the 1830s when he was recuperating from yellow fever. He and his family renovated and made several additions to the old house. It is said that Farquhar, who had been an English professor as well as a medical doctor, liked the name Olney because he admired the poems and hymns of William Cowper (1731-1800). Cowper lived in Olney, England, where he and John Newton, a minister, composed many hymns that were published in 1779 as "The Olney Hymns."

Local lore suggests that Dr. Farquhar was responsible for the name change, but he died in 1844, several years before the name "Olney" was selected. Roger Brooke Farquhar (grandson of Dr. Farquhar) in *Old Homes and History of Montgomery County, Maryland,* (1962) noted that his widowed grandmother, Sarah, was not pleased with the town's new name. "When the name was changed to Olney, it is reported that the widow, Sarah B. Farquhar, did not desire to have the name of her home thus publicized," he wrote.

It took many years for residents to forget the name, Mechanicsville. Even the 1879 G.M. Hopkins map lists both names -- Mechanicsville and underneath it the words, Olney P.O.

Postal records show the existence of the Olney Post Office as early as 1851. The records also mention that Jonathan D. Barnsley became postmaster in 1853. That year his salary was reported to be $28.71. Until the mid-1900s the post office was always in one of the general stores in the village.

Historical documents indicate that Jonathan Barnsley had purchased a general store in 1837. This could have been Benedict Duley's old store, the first one that opened in the village. There is an intriguing reference in J. Thomas Scharf's *History of Western Maryland* (1882) that no liquor was sold in the store after Jonathan became the owner.

Jonathan, like most general store owners, kept a wide variety of items. Roger Brooke Farquhar's book includes his grandmother's records of 1851 and 1852 that list the following items purchased in the general store: "ten lbs. sugar @ 70 cents; 1 lb. coffee @ 14 cents; pair of shoes for Ellen @ 75 cents; one-half gal. of molasses, 20 cents."

Like most general storeowners Jonathan was the unofficial banker as well as grocer for the farming families in the community. According to letters written at that time, Jonathan gave credit to farmers until they could sell their products and accepted farm products in barter for goods in his store. Occasionally Jonathan even paid farm laborers when a farmer's cash was tied up. The farmer would reimburse the store keeper after the harvest.

Letters also indicate that Jonathan provided other services to the farming community. One letter requested that he permit a young woman to spend the night at his residence so that she could catch the early morning stage.

Another requested him to supply "a nice little coffin for my infant child, two months old and a half. You will oblige by having it here by 2 o'clock tomorrow afternoon, as we propose to have the funeral at 3 p.m." Jonathan later charged $30 for the coffin and for the care of the man's wife.

Although J. Thomas Scharf's *History of Western Maryland* (1882) notes there was a tavern in Mechanicsville in 1830, very little additional information about the establishment is known. However more tantalizing tidbits about Higgins Tavern, located on Georgia Avenue about two miles south of the crossroads, have been recorded. Tax assessment records for 1829 indicate that Lucretia Beall owned the "Tavern Stand" on an improved lot. The tavern is mentioned again in a suit for unpaid debts lodged against Thomas Higgins. In defending himself Higgins said he had spent his money on improvements to the tavern. Lucretia denied knowledge of Higgins' debts and claimed that she had made the improvements on the tavern. She also said that Higgins had lived with her for 20 years and that he acted as her agent for land purchases. In fact, Higgins had purchased over 120 acres adjoining the tavern property and had signed the property over to Lucretia.

In 1856 the case was settled with the finding that Higgins owned no property. However Higgins did not get to enjoy his victory, as he was dead by the time the case was settled. Lucretia kept the tavern.

An 1865 map notes that H.O. Higgins operated a hotel at the site. How he relates to Lucretia Beall and Thomas Higgins is unclear. However two years later Lucretia sold the tavern and some adjacent acreage to Margaret Higgins, H. O. Higgins' wife. The only other reference to the tavern occurred in 1872 when a public meeting for Democratic candidates was held there. Since there is no further mention of the tavern, it is assumed that the tavern ceased operating during the next few years. There is no listing of the site on the G. M. Hopkins 1879 map.

Through the years the tavern has been significantly altered. Today the building, located by the Silo Inn, is used as a retail shop.

By the 1870s Olney was thriving. Competition among the artisans and shop owners must have been robust. On the 1879 G.M. Hopkins map, there were two general stores under separate "Business Notices" -- J.D. Barnsley and Williams & Boyer. Joseph L. Wagner, was listed as a "manufacturer and dealer in stoves, tin and sheet iron ware also roofing, etc." Other documents showed blacksmiths, carpenters, a butcher, wheelwright, physician, tailor and a machinist located in Olney. Farms of various sizes surrounded the town.

In *History of Montgomery County 1879*, T.H.S. Boyd described Olney as having good land. Since agriculture provided the livelihood for most residents, Boyd listed land values by the crops the land produced. The land was valued "at forty dollars per acre," he wrote and yielded "25 bushels of Wheat, 50 of Corn, and 1200 pounds of Tobacco. Churches and School convenient. Population, 75." At the time Boyd wrote his historical account, Episcopalians had established St. John's Episcopal Church, and the county had just built a public school. Several private schools had been organized in the Olney-Sandy Spring area.

Although Olney had all the ingredients of a town, many residents, especially Quakers, looked to Sandy Spring for cultural and spiritual leadership. Boyd described Sandy Spring in 1879 as having "land under a high state of cultivation, and improved by handsome buildings." Two businesses still operating today were founded in Sandy Spring -- The Montgomery Mutual Insurance Company in 1844 and the Sandy Spring National Bank in 1868.

The Quaker community also formed the Sandy Spring Lyceum Company in 1858 to hold lectures and other activities. Members of the company, including a few non-Quakers, were "desirous of improving their minds while cultivating their farms," wrote William Henry Farquhar in vol. 1 of the *Sandy Spring Annals.*

Although Charles F. Brooke described the Olney of the 1800s as "a dingy old place," he noted improved conditions in the community after the Civil War. "...Improvement set in, and with energy, thrift, new buildings and paint, we have the Olney of today," he said in 1926.

Chapter 4

THE FARMERS' GREATEST GIFT

The farming economy fueled the growth of early Olney, but the farmers left an even more important mark on the village. The biggest contribution made, replied one long-time farmer was "the self-help the farmers gave each other through the old farmers' club." Describing the dozen or so farmers that got together in 1844 to form a club he said, "The farmers around here were a right progressive bunch." They met and visited each other's farm operation, discussed problems and came up with solutions. They shared knowledge about their experiments for the mutual benefit of everyone in the farming community.

Prior to the days of refrigeration and motorized vehicles, farmers found innovative solutions to the problems that confronted them -- repairing rutted dirt roads, bringing the harvest to market, storing ice for the summer. They did it through the local farmers clubs. The Olney Grange, a local chapter of a national farming organization, even lobbied for a nationwide parcel post system after hearing complaints from farmers about package delivery.

THE FARM ECONOMY

From the beginning the farm economy spawned the growth of small Maryland villages. In Olney the wheelwright made wheels for wagons and wheelbarrows; a blacksmith repaired farming tools and shod horses; a tinsmith soldered milk buckets and repaired roofs of houses and barns.

Artisans who had set up shops at the crossroads also provided a central location where farmers could learn the latest news about the community. Today it seems strange that the towns of Brookeville and Sandy Spring, both within three miles of Olney, also had artisans to serve the nearby farms. One wonders how all the artisans were supported by the farming community. Back then, farming was an even more rigorous livelihood than it is today. And a horse, which for so many years was the mainstay of farming, could only walk about three miles an hour with a heavy load. Farmers were glad to have the services they needed as nearby as possible.

FARMING IN THE 1700s AND 1800s

he first settlers planted tobacco as the main cash crop, the common currency of the Maryland province. Farmers used tobacco to purchase items, pay off debts and settle fines that were levied for disobeying laws.

Olney's nearness to Washington also affected its agriculture and trade. Initially farmers rolled hogsheads filled with tobacco to ports like Elkridge Landing on the Patapsco River and later Georgetown where ships waited for the cargo. By the early 1800s Olney area farmers used wagons to haul their crop, a round trip that took about two days to Georgetown.

But problems developed in these early farming communities, and eventually farmers left the area in search of more fertile soil. One bad period began after the Revolutionary War when there was an increased demand for tobacco. The settlers had already grown the weed for many years, and cultivating tobacco wreaked havoc on the soil. It robbed the soil of nitrogen and potash. Poor farming methods did not replenish these nutrients, and the soil had become worn-out. Following the demand there was a glut of tobacco on the market. Prices dropped. By the early 1800s there were good markets for produce in Baltimore and Washington, but the farmers had no easy way to travel there. The combination of these headaches forced many farmers to leave the county and head west to purchase farmland. "Agriculture began to languish; old fields, abandoned to broom sedge, became the most striking feature of the rural landscape," wrote William Henry Farquhar in 1863 in volume I of *The Annals of Sandy Spring*.

The Quaker farmers of Sandy Spring decided something should be done to reverse the downhill trend of farming. Several resourceful farmers pooled their ideas, which led the way to methods of soil revitalization. One technique was growing other crops, and by 1879 corn was edging out tobacco as the largest crop in the county.

Although never as important as tobacco, wheat, too, was a cash crop in the late 1700s. As early as 1737 Sandy Spring's James Brooke and John Thomas had constructed a wheat flour mill -- one of the first in the state -- near what is today Gold Mine Road. It was fitting that when Richard, James' son who built Fair Hill around 1760 joined the militia during the Revolutionary War, he was given the job of collecting wheat from the farmers in the county. The grain was taken to a Georgetown mill where it was ground into flour to be stored and distributed as needed.

THOMAS MOORE -- AGRICULTURAL PIONEER

Considered one of the most innovative farmers of his time, Thomas Moore made several notable contributions to improving farming techniques. He also counted some distinguished figures among his friends. Articles and historic accounts indicate that Moore shared a friendship with both Thomas Jefferson and James Madison.

In *Chronicles of Sandy Spring Friends Meeting and Environs* (1987), Martha C. Nesbitt provides a tantalizing story about Moore's marriage to Mary Brooke, a granddaughter of James. Moore, born in Waterford, Virginia in 1760, was a tenant at James Brooke's farmstead in 1784. By 1791 Nesbitt notes the young man had captivated Mary's heart. Following their marriage, the newlyweds set up housekeeping in a six-room log cabin. The farm, located on property that had belonged to her late father, Roger, was on the west side of Georgia Avenue about two miles north of the Olney intersection. The young couple named their farm Retreat. A few years later Mary inherited the property.

Historic records indicate that the soil at the Moore's 280-acres homestead was considered poor for cultivation, so Moore put his scientific mind to work. He performed agricultural experiments and employed innovative techniques that enhanced the soil and increased its productivity. Some of the ideas that Moore introduced included adding manure and plaster of paris, deep plowing, sowing clover, and rotating crops.

According to local histories, Moore corresponded with both President Thomas Jefferson and then Secretary of State James Madison about the results of his experiments. Articles noted that when Thomas Jefferson brought a mold board plow from France, a new invention that both dug into and turned the soil, he brought it to Moore's farm where it was first operated. Farmers from near and far visited Retreat to experience first-hand the results of Moore's agricultural experiments.

Moore was an extremely industrious and gifted individual. He was an accomplished engineer, author and a skilled inventor as shown in the invention of the first icebox. Before refrigeration, some farmers cut ice from the ponds during the winter months and stored the solid blocks in a hold covered with straw. As an innovator, Moore took this idea a step further. He experimented with keeping butter cold, and in 1803 his tests led him to develop a refrigerator for which he received the first patent. The patent was signed by then President Thomas Jefferson who also served as Commissioner of Patents.

Moore's refrigerator was described by J. Thomas Scharf in the *History of Western Maryland* (1882).

> "The refrigerator consisted of a cedar tub of oval form, and [was] about eighteen or twenty inches deep; in this was placed a tin box with the corners square, which would contain twenty-two prints of butter of one pound each, leaving space on each side between the tin and the wood for ice in small lumps. The outside of the wooden box was covered with rabbit-skin with the fur on, and over that was a covering of coarse woolen cloth. In this first refrigerator the butter was carried on horseback to the market at Georgetown, D.C., a distance of twenty miles, in warm weather, hard and firm, and with ice enough left to give each purchaser a small lump."

A print of butter is butter that has been molded in a form like a small wooden box that holds one pound. One end of the form has a decorative design that is pressed into the butter during the molding process.

Moore's refrigerator attracted some attention among residents of Washington. "Thomas Jefferson, then President of the United States, some of the heads of departments, and other citizens of the District of Columbia, who had ice-houses, used Thomas Moore's patent refrigerators," wrote Scharf. However the patent expired 14 years later and Moore did not renew it. The device never gained widespread popularity because many farmers did not have icehouses.

Moore's engineering projects included laying out the National Road that ran from Cumberland, Md., to Ohio in 1806. In 1809 Moore was elected to the Philadelphia Agricultural Society and is said to have been the only Montgomery County resident to receive this honor.

In 1799 Moore and his brother-in-law Isaac Briggs, a local resident, founded the Sandy Spring Farmers' Society. The organization was established to share agricultural information among the farming community and to promote scientific inquiry and advancement in the agricultural field. James Madison was named an Honorary Corresponding member in 1802 because of his keen interest in promoting agriculture. Moore wrote several books on farming topics. He authored *The Great Error of American Agriculture Exposed and Hints for Improvement Suggested*, which was printed in 1801 and was the first publication of the society.

Moore and his wife Mary lived in their cabin at Retreat for many years. Moore's nephew, Thomas McCormick, spent some of his childhood years with his uncle at Retreat but later went to Baltimore to learn the craft of carpentry. In 1817 Moore summoned his nephew to build a colonial brick house at his homestead. McCormick built a two-and-one-half story residence that was symmetrical in design, and flanked with a wing on each side of a center section that gave the house a T-shape. The house was considered classical in appearance and typical of manor homes built in the region during that period, but had distinctive inverted U-shaped chimney caps.

Just five years later, in 1822, Thomas Moore died. In 1829 Mc-Cormick purchased the residence from Moore's widow, Mary. McCormick changed the name to Longwood, supposedly after a black mahogany tree that grew on the property. The tree was said to have come from St. Helena, the island where Napoleon was exiled. The present Longwood Recreation Center is located on part of the Longwood tract.

Although the house called Longwood is a gracious private residenace on a quiet cul-de-sac, the structure bears little resemblace to the original. The mansion sits on almost two acres amid towering horse chestnut trees, magnolias and mature evergreens. The Longwood mansion is one of the few remaining structures that reflects Olney's past. Listed on the Maryland register of historic places, Longwood is within walking distance of Longwood Recreation Center.

BENJAMIN HALLOWELL -- HEAD OF FIRST MARYLAND AGRICULTURAL COLLEGE

Early in life, Benjamin Hallowell earned a reputation as a leading educator and lecturer. In later years, he also made contributions to the progress of agriculture in the Olney farming community.

In 1842 Hallowell retired from teaching and running a boy's boarding school in Alexandria, Virginia. He was only 43. He returned to his farm in Olney to begin farming full time. His reason for retiring strikes a familiar chord for many in the work world today but also demonstrates the breadth of his knowledge. "The wear of the large school, my lecturing twice a week, through nearly the whole term of eleven months, on Natural Philosophy, Chemistry, Astronomy, Geology, and Vegetable and Animal Physiology...began to tell unfavorably on my physical constitution," he wrote in *Autobiography of Benjamin Hallowell* (1884).

PHOTO 5 An old photograph shows Rockland, the home of Benjamin Hallowell. After Hallowell died, his son used the house for the Rockland School. In the late 1980s the house was renovated, and now a housing development is located on the land that Hallowell once farmed. Photo courtesy of the Sandy Spring Museum.

Hallowell had an intense love of nature. In his autobiography Hallowell recounted his interest which began as a young man. "When at leisure,...I rambled into the woods and among the flowers and irrigating streams in what had been grandfather's back meadow." Continuing he wrote, "I was very fond of watching and listening to the birds, observing the waves on the growing grain...All nature pleased me."

In his book Hallowell provided a glimpse of farm life in Olney. Describing how he tried to reclaim an unproductive meadow by planting timothy, a type of grass used for hay, he wrote "I commenced ditching, underdraining, and removing the bushes and rocks from eight acres of meadow land...and had it plowed and prepared for seeding in timothy in the fall." Hallowell invested $136 for manures and work on the project. His neighbors thought he had spent far too much and said that Hallowell had wasted his money. But Hallowell's investment paid off and he had the last laugh. "I sold in each of the two succeeding years more from that meadow than the whole improvement cost me," he wrote.

In the fall of 1843, Hallowell returned to education. He accepted a position to teach chemistry at Columbian College in Washington, D.C. While teaching there he was introduced to a celebrated agriculturist, John S. Skinner who stopped by to pay Hallowell a visit. "The object of his visit," Hallowell wrote, "was to get me to tell the composition of two powders from Germany, which were said to be a certain remedy for the murrain in cattle, as he was writing a treatise on cattle disease, he very much wished to know of what it was composed." Hallowed provided Skinner with the chemical analysis of the remedy, and Skinner spoke highly of Hallowell's scientific achievements. Hallowell received credit for his accomplishment of the analysis in a book Skinner later wrote. Hallowell's reputation as an educator and scientist gave him no peace. His skills were continually sought by others. In 1845 he reluctantly accepted the position as principal of a Friends School in Philadelphia that was about to be established. But in his autobiography Hallowell said that what he wanted most was a quiet, retired, country life to till the soil and plant crops.

Officials in Maryland also recognized Hallowell's many talents. In 1856 the state legislature established the Agricultural College and Model Farm. The purpose of the college was to provide agricultural instruction and research. Hallowell was asked to provide his views on the location, objects and aims of the institution. Again the educator found himself in the lead and wrote, "I was unanimously elected President of this Agricultural College." The first classes began in September of that year, and the college eventually became the Agricultural College of the University of Maryland.

But Hallowell never stopped returning to his love -- country life and farming at his Rockland homestead in Olney. In 1844 Hallowell and Richard Bentley, a well-known Sandy Spring farmer, founded the Farmers Club of Sandy Spring. The two Quakers recognized that farmers needed to support each other and share solutions to common problems. While there may have been one or two farmer's clubs established earlier in the state, none lasted as long nor was as strong as the Sandy Spring group. The Farmers Club of Sandy Spring still meets today.

Hallowell's Rockland farm no longer exists but his house still stands. His former residence, which has been renovated, is surrounded by modern colonial homes and townhouses in a subdivision that bears his name.

THE OLNEY GRANGE

Hallowell and Bentley were ahead of their time. By 1867 farmers nationwide realized they could benefit by banding together to help themselves. This feeling of self-help kept the local farmers clubs going and was probably the impetus for state and national farming organizations.

The National Grange began in 1867, and local chapters formed soon after. In 1873 Joseph Moore, a member of one of the Sandy Spring farmers' clubs, helped establish Olney Grange #7. The grange was actually begun about a month before the founding of the State Grange which was established in 1874.

Farmers flocked to the new grange, and membership had to be restricted to farmers that lived within a 3.5 mile radius of Olney. A grange hall was erected on the southeast side of Georgia Avenue at the intersection of what is today Georgia Avenue and Route 108. The members met on the second Tuesday afternoon of the month. They heard lectures on food for dairy stock, talked about cooperative buying and marketing and exchanged agricultural information. Members discussed community needs and held family dinners at the hall. Since the grange had a large meeting room, other community groups used the facility for concerts and events. An entry in the Sandy Spring Annals for January 1896 reads, "The Olney Grange entertained the county grange and discussed a set of text books for public school. The grange hall was used for dances through winter given by Olney Dance Club."

One of the greatest success stories of Olney Grange #7 involved the Parcel Post system. According to Mary and Eben Jenkins authors of *The First Hundred Years, Maryland State Grange 1874-1974* (1974), the National Grange had lobbied the federal government to include packages in its mail service for many years. But legislation was always blocked by private package delivery businesses. At a meeting in January 1911 Olney grange members planned to wage a forceful campaign for the legislation. They decided to lobby and write letters to congressional candidates. Members wrote to their Congressional representatives to persuade them to establish a parcel post service, and were eager to support a candidate in the upcoming election that would support parcel post legislation. One member of the Olney group, Reuben Brigham, became the leader of the effort.

Brigham met with candidate David J. Lewis many times about the farmer's need for the service. "Brigham attended the Parcel Post conference in Washington April 25, 1911, and 'found encouragement there for their pet reform' [parcel post legislation]," wrote the Jenkins. Lewis supported the legislation and the grange threw its support behind Lewis in the 1911 congressional race. "David J. Lewis (Sixth Maryland District) was elected to Congress and became the 'Father' of the parcel Post Law he sponsored," the authors wrote. Lewis led the congressional fight for the parcel post service and later credited Brigham and the Olney Grange for bringing the matter to his attention. Congress approved the legislation for the Parcel Post in 1912 and the service began in January 1913. Brigham often visited Congressman Lewis in Washington. They forged a lasting friendship and Brigham named his son David L. after the congressman.

The Olney Grange operated for 96 years. Finally, the charter was given up in 1969, although the grange hall had been sold many years earlier. In 1936 the old grange building was renovated and became the D.G.S. Grocery Store. The building was demolished in the late 1970s when the Olney intersection was widened.

THE HOME FRONT

Houses in the 18th century were often small. Richard K. Mac-Master and Ray Eldon Hiebert described the typical early farm house in the region in *A Grateful Remembrance, the Story of Montgomery County* 1976. "...it was a low, one- or two-room cabin with a sharply pitched roof extended to cover a narrow porch...The log house was covered sometimes by plank; less frequently, it was a brick or stone structure." The authors explained that farms often had a log barn near the house as well as one or more log tobacco houses. The tobacco houses were modified with large gaps between the logs so the tobacco could be air-dried.

As families became more prosperous, their houses were enlarged or torn down to build larger residences. A perfect example from the 1800s is today's Olney House. When Whitson Canby lived in the house, it was a small log structure. In the 1840s subsequent owners, Sarah and Charles Farquhar, enlarged the dwelling with several additions.

Woodburn, an historic house on Batchellors Forest Road was another Olney area home that was originally built as a log cabin. The Mahlon Kirk family lived in the simple cabin, probably in the 1840s, and made an addition. In the 1880s another member of the family added a wing, and in the 1930s, other owners made extensive renovations to the original log cabin.

Other Olney farmers started over when they outgrew their original houses. One example is the Longwood house. Thomas and Mary Brooke Moore began their married life in a six-room log cabin, Retreat, mentioned earlier in this chapter. They remained in the house for more than 25 years before building a two and one-half story brick house in 1817.

In earlier years families were more self-reliant for the necessities of everyday life. The ready-made food items of today could not be purchased at the general store. Women's work was tedious. They spent hours baking bread in a brick oven; killing, cleaning and stewing chickens; curing ham or bacon; picking and preparing the vegetables to last through the winter; and making herbal remedies for illnesses.

Other than a broom fashioned from corn husks, there weren't many household gadgets to make cleaning the house easier. This, too, was back-breaking work. Like the farmers who helped each other with agricultural problems, women shared their experiences to help each other out. Elizabeth Ellicott Lea, a young Sandy Spring widow who ran a 200-acre farm, chose to assist other housewives by writing down her solutions to household problems. In 1845 she wrote a cookbook *Domestic Cookery, Useful Receipts and Hints to Young Housekeepers*, to assist young inexperienced housewives cope with their numerous household tasks. She found an eager audience as the book went through 19 printings.

Lea kept her instructions simple and to the point. "In boiling fresh meat, care is necessary to have the water boiling all the time it is in the pot," she wrote. Lea also advised housewives on other problems that might befall them. Each week during the summer months, Lea recommended that they search and brush the bedsteads for bed-bugs. "If they are infested with bugs," Lea wrote, "boil the sacking in lye and water, or put it in an oven, on some boards, after the bread is taken out, to kill the eggs." Such was the work of women during an earlier period in history.

TRANSPORTATION

The farmers' ability to solve their own problems is graphically illustrated by how they tackled the road system, or more accurately, the lack of a road system. During the 18th century, roads were barely cleared dirt paths or old Indian trails. The poor condition of roads was not peculiar to Maryland. In a paper on transportation and travel, a local historian wrote, "Thomas Jefferson, as President, when he went home from Washington to Monticello (Virginia), though he rode in a coach with four horses, undertook a journey that required a week of travel." Of course travel by coach and horses was slightly more comfortable than riding horseback, but not everyone owned a coach. In the Olney area, it was more likely that citizens traveled on horseback or in a wagon.

It's hard to imagine how difficult and time-consuming it was to transport farm goods a mere 18 to 20 miles in the 18th, 19th and early 20th century, when, today, airlines leave the east coast and arrive on the west coast in a few hours. Eighty years ago it took Olney farmers about the same time to take a load of hay 18 miles to Washington as it does to arrive on the opposite coast today. Today's farmers estimate that a farmer could average four to six miles an hour when trotting on horseback, or about three miles an hour with a heavy load because the horses had to walk.

Farmers in Montgomery County worked hard to develop techniques to improve land production during the 1800s. But the markets for produce and hay in Baltimore and Washington were still not easily accessible. One long-time resident wrote a paper about local transit and noted that transportation, or lack of it, has always been a problem in this part of Maryland. The writer quoted a Baltimore friend who stated in the 1860s, "I can make a trip to Europe more easily than one to Sandy Spring."

PHOTO 6 This stagecoach went from Sandy Spring to Laurel. There was probably a similar vehicle that served Olney. Photo courtesy of the Sandy Spring Museum.

A local area resident who tried his hand at improving transportation was quite successful. Allen Bowie Davis (1809-1889) owned the Greenwood estate of more than 1,000 acres which was located north of Brookeville. Davis organized the Union Turnpike Company which was established in 1849 to build a toll road from Brookeville to the Seventh Street Pike in Washington. In contrast to today's sophisticated highway building methods, the turnpike construction of the mid 1800s simply consisted of widening and resurfacing many of the old dirt beds. But it was still an improvement over the old roads that were used to haul produce to Washington. The company also built connecting roads to Sandy Spring and Ashton. Today, Bowie's Washington Brookeville Turnpike is called Georgia Avenue.

Old turnpikes were surfaced in a number of ways. Some turnpikes had a layer of large stones placed on the dirt that were covered by a second layer of smaller stones to harden the road. Other turnpikes had planks of wood laid down over the soil. The hard surface in some sections of the tollroads was only wide enough for one vehicle. One wagon would pull off and out of the way on the dirt section or strip alongside the hard surface when meeting another wagon. One resident explained that the heavily loaded wagons typically remained on the hard surface and a buggy or carriage would take to the mud or dust of the dirt alongside the road.

Toll booths were placed along the routes to pay for the construction and upkeep of the roads. The Olney toll booth was located on the southwest side of the Georgia Avenue/Route 108 intersection. In later years the tinsmith, whose house and shop were located at that corner, collected the tolls. Historic accounts indicate that tolls ranged from two cents per mile for wagons pulled by two animals to 25 cents for a score of cattle.

Some toll booths charged according to the width of the wagon wheel. A narrow wheel would cost more than a wide wheel because the wide tire would roll down more dirt and keep the road more level while the narrow wheel would make more ruts. The tolls helped to keep the roads in passable condition.

There was no actual gate that blocked the road at the toll booth. The youth of that generation liked to tease the toll collector and get away without paying the toll. According to local lore, in the late 1800s, young men would throw stones at the guard's booth at night to wake him or to get his attention. Once the collector was aware that someone was passing through, the young men would quickly go by without paying the toll and would delight in their accomplishment. The turnpike was sold to the State of Maryland in 1914 and the Union Turnpike Company was dissolved.

Before modern paving methods became prevalent, there were three types of roads: turnpikes, country and private roads. Harold B. Stabler in *Some Recollections and Anecdotes and Tales of Old Times* (1962) said the latter two were mostly dirt.

"Only here and there were they surfaced with stone...in order to keep them from becoming impassible in winter," Stabler wrote. He explained that dirt roads were usually satisfactory and could be used in dry weather if the dust were not deep, but they were likely to be terrible during the winter. The method of transportation also compensated, to some degree, for roads of that period Stabler said. "But horses, mules, and oxen could slowly drag vehicles through deep mud where automobiles and trucks, had they existed, would have been perfectly helpless, and would have bogged down immediately."

Even into the 1920s, the farming community continued their practice of self-help to solve their problems. A local farmer recalled the community effort to keep the dirt roads passable. "Every year in the field where we were going to mow hay over with sickle bars we'd tie a burlap bag around our waist, take hold of the corners, and we'd go over the field and pick up stones," he said. "We'd haul them in a wagon and dump them along the road and there would be men with what were called stone hammers, and if the stone was big enough to break up, they'd break that

stone up and fill in the muddy places along the different roads."
This "patch work" helped so the wagons, and in the early twentieth
century the newfangled vehicles, wouldn't get mired in the mud.

Until around 1912 when automobiles and buses came into their
own there was no rapid transit connection from the Olney area.
In a paper describing the plight of those who lived in the area one
resident wrote, "During all this time, the chief means of
travel...was individually owned horses hitched to dogcarts, bug-
gies, traps, carryalls, daytons and carriages, not to mention the
two-, four- and six- horse teams that hauled the wagon loads of
farm products first to Georgetown and Elkridge Landing and
later to Laurel, Ellicott City, Washington and Baltimore."

When residents from Sandy Spring needed a ride into
Washington they hitched a ride on a dairy wagon that was going
into the city. With the advent of cars and trucks R. R. Moore of
Sandy Spring started a truck route that accommodated pas-
sengers who didn't mind sitting on milk cans. Olney resident
Leonard Burns opened a bus and truck line in 1914, and continued the service for about 10 years.

FARMING FROM 1900 TO 1950

Farming revolved around horses up until the early 1930s one local
farmer said. Tractors were not used until early to mid 1930s he
explained.

Another farmer described the typical farms of this era. Almost all
farmers had turkeys, chickens, cows, hogs, and some dairy cattle.
Wheat, corn, barley, oats, rye and hay were raised along with
vegetables. Part of the corn and hay crop was used to feed the
livestock. The wheat was hauled by a four-horse team to a local
mill to be ground.

Washington was a good market for the produce and hay of local
farmers. Hay was hauled in large wagons until about 1916. One
farmer said, "I can remember hauling loose hay, big wagon loads
of loose hay loaded on and 'poled down' (held in place by a pole).

PHOTO 7 Stanley Stabler of Brookeville rides an antique wheat binder that is pulled by a team of horses. The binder was used in the 1920s and 1930s. The binder cut the wheat and tied it in bundles that were dropped to the ground. Farm hands then put eight or ten bundles together in a shock. The shocks were loaded onto wagons and taken to the threshing machine, which separated the wheat from the straw. Photo courtesy of Mark D. Faram.

They'd be 18-20 feet long and 10-12 feet wide, a great big mound of hay...and you'd take that down to the Washington market where it would be sold to people who had horses for carriages and delivery wagons."

The farmers would leave the Olney area between midnight and 2 a.m. and travel south on Georgia Avenue to Washington's 7th Street market. The trip might take six hours if hay was hauled because the horses could only walk with such a large load. Lighter loads of produce would take a little less time because the horses could travel a little faster. Farmers tried to be to market by 4 a.m. That was when the customers arrived to purchase the best the farmers had to offer, and the hucksters came to load up their wagons and begin door-to-door sales routes in the neighborhoods. On a good market day a farmer might be finished by 7 a.m. and ready to head home with his team of horses and wagon.

Around 1920 trucks began replacing horse-drawn wagons. A local bus service began a trucking company to serve the farming community. The trucks hauled the farmers' cattle, grain or produce to market. One truck was dedicated to picking up milk cans from the dairy farms and taking them to one of the nearby dairies where the milk was bottled and delivered to homes.

Farmers were ingenious in finding ways to make ends meet. Some farmers bought 10 to 20 steers in the fall. They fed them in the winter and spring, then sold them to dealers in the area or took them back to Baltimore the following year to the cattle market. Other farmers took fresh turkeys, chickens, eggs and vegetables they didn't need for their families and sold them along regular routes. They headed downtown toward Washington and lower Montgomery County where the more developed communities no longer had nearby farms to purchase fresh poultry, eggs and produce.

THE WASHINGTON CONNECTION

Although Olney's farming community served many Washington residents, its idyllic setting also attracted prominent people who worked in the congested city. Two residents, L. C. Probert (1883-1937) and Harold Ickes (1874-1952) associated with presidents, and each man earn his place in history. Curiously enough, both men owned the same farm on Route 108 west of the Olney intersection at different times.

By the time Probert bought Homeland Farm in the mid-1920s, he had won respect in two fields, railroads and newspapers. Born in New York, he work as a day laborer and a locomotive fireman before joining the Buffalo Express as a newspaper reporter.

As a young reporter Probert probably got his first experience covering presidents when he attended the public reception held by President William McKinley (president 1897-1901) in Buffalo on Sept. 6, 1901. Little did anyone realize that McKinley would be assassinated later that day.

Probert joined the Associated Press service in 1905 as a reporter and worked his way up the ladder to news editor and bureau chief. He headed the Washington Bureau from 1918 to 1927. As head of the bureau he went to Paris with President Woodrow Wilson (president 1913-1921) to cover the Paris Peace Conference that ended World War I.

While Probert was covering the nation's leaders, his wife Adelaide settled in Olney community life. But tragedy struck soon after they moved to the farm. The house, built in 1840, burned and very little could be done to save it. There is an undocumented story that the local fire department's newly-purchased fire engine ran out of gas en route to the fire.

Another story says that President Calvin Coolidge (president 1923-1929) offered to let Probert stay in the White House after the house fire. But Probert refused because of his position at the Associated Press.

Probert rebuilt the house and there is evidence that he customized a Sears Roebuck house to fit his needs. Soon after the fire Probert resigned from the Associated Press and went back to the railroad industry. He became vice president of the Chesapeake and Ohio Railroad. Several longtime residents said the famous symbol that signifies the railroad, the sleeping cat, originated at the newly-built Homeland Farm.

According to the story an artist visited Probert to discuss the creation of a symbol and logo. As the artist was leaving, he saw a kitten asleep beside one of the six massive columns on the front porch. The sleeping kitten became the logo for the Chesapeake and Ohio Railroad.

Probert died in 1937 leaving no heirs, and Homeland Farm was placed on the market. The new owner, Harold Ickes, would become even closer to a head of state. Ickes entertained President Franklin D. Roosevelt at the 270-acre farm and witnessed a part of the president's private life not often recounted in popular histories.

Ickes served as Roosevelt's Secretary of the Interior beginning in 1933 and invited numerous Washington officials to the farm. He led the department in a new direction and became one of the most forward thinking conservationists of his time. Later, during World War II, Roosevelt appointed Ickes as his petroleum administrator.

In Volume Two, *The Secret Diary of Harold L. Ickes* (1953-54) the interior secretary described the farm, "as a perfectly lovely place." Ickes and his second wife, Jane, renamed their home Headwaters Farm.

Jane managed the daily chores at the farm. She developed a large chicken and egg operation. Due to the demands of his job, Ickes was only able to help out in his spare time, and he specialized in vegetable and flower gardening. Some residents still recall the fragrant peonies, bright spring daffodils and striking dahlias in the gardens.

In *Righteous Pilgrim: The Life and Times of Harold L. Ickes*, (1990) T.H. Watkins described the farm as having, "five hundred capons, one thousand laying hens, two thousand pullets, and four thousand chicks occupying eight poultry houses and two brooding sheds." There were also cows, pigs, sheep, a cornfield, a wheat field, (and) flower gardens..." But according to Watkins, "the farm never did make much money, in spite of Jane's exhausting labors."

Some nearby residents of the area tried to keep up with the comings and goings of Secretary Ickes. Volume V of the *Annals of Sandy Spring* for the year 1938 records, "December 21st, President Franklin D. Roosevelt, took dinner at The Headwaters Farm with Secy and Mrs. Ickes." What residents didn't know was that Roosevelt visited Ickes a number of times for poker parties. The betting limit was usually $1. In Volume Two of his diary Ickes wrote, "these parties at my house always go off very well. The President comes early. We have a good dinner and then, unless the weather is too warm, we play poker in the living room with the fire going in the open grate." Ickes added that two of the regular guests, "insist that these parties go off better at my house than even at the White House." While describing the parties Ickes told of the beer and whiskeys he served and said the president, "was quite fond of beer."

Headwaters Farm adds a distinctive historic feature to Olney, especially to the community where the Ickes residence is located. The road off Route 108 leading into the subdivision bears the name of the old Ickes Farm. Today the former Ickes mansion has been restored and is a private residence.

TODAY

Farming -- earning a livelihood off the land -- permeates the history of the Olney area and Montgomery County. But times have changed and people have changed, and all these changes have impinged on the farming industry.

The retirement or death of many Olney area farmers of the mid-1900s left farming in the hands of their heirs. Younger generations often look for vastly different lifestyles than their parents. More career choices are available today than they were in earlier periods of history and frequently the offspring of farmers want something different. Often they have no desire nor love of tilling the soil for a lifetime, and few area families have remained in farming.

Although the reasons for ending a family farming enterprise may change with each family, the reasons for selling a farm tend to be a story that is often retold. The case of dairy farmer John M. Beane who owned and farmed land that ran along the east side of Georgia Avenue and the south side of Route 108 is a typical one. When he died, his wife and son rented the land to another local farmer who used it to pasture his Angus cattle.

As growth spread farther into upper Montgomery County from over-developed areas in the lower section, farms were sought by developers. Beane's farm was sold, and the local farmer who had rented the land for his cows had to sell the animals because he had no convenient place to put them to pasture. The developers replaced the waving fields of grain with subdivisions, and today the old Beane farm is the subdivision of Hallowell.

As some variation of this story became commonplace, county officials became worried over the swelling sales of farmland to developers. In 1980 a pilot program to preserve the surrounding farmland was developed and put into the Olney Master Plan.

Under the program farmers whose land was placed in the agricultural preserve were awarded transfer development rights (TDRs). One TDR was given for each five acres the farmer owned on which there was no house. If he owned 100 acres, he would get 20 TDRs.

The TDRs had a monetary value. The farmer could sell them to developers. Special receiving areas where TDRs could be applied were designated in the Olney Master Plan. The developer could purchase TDRs and use them in these specially designated areas to increase the density and build more houses than the base zoning requirements permitted. The farmer could use the money for improving his farm. Later, the preservation program was extended to other areas of the county.

Today, little of Olney's farming heritage remains. The intersection no longer houses the wheelwright and tinsmith shops to serve the farming community. The blacksmith remains although he has adapted his business to include small engine repair as well as blacksmithing and welding.

What was once a farming village crossroads is now a hectic intersection where residents pause as they travel to and from work and errands. The businesses in the area reflect the changes too. Several restaurants and busy take-out eateries cater to working families who make quick stops to gather the foodstuffs for a family meal.

Although the signs of a farming heritage are gone, the sense of community and self-help remain strong. Local organizations plan community events and fight for their share of schools and roads. Like the farmers of yesteryear, the residents can be described as a, "right progressive bunch." Perhaps like a good crop, some of the values handed down from farmers years ago remain.

Chapter 5

THE CIVIL WAR: A COMMUNITY DIVIDED

Residents of Olney, like those in surrounding communities, struggled with the issues of the day -- slavery, abolition, secession and war. Within the village neighbors were split in their allegiance to the north or south.

Large landowners near Olney and other villages depended upon slaves for farm help. Many had southern family ties and sympathized with the Confederate cause. The Quaker community in nearby Sandy Spring had strong convictions against slavery and for the most part sympathized with the Union. Several influential Quakers like Benjamin Hallowell lived in Olney.

The turmoil within the state was so great that some residents advocated secession. During 1860 Maryland went through a secession crisis that continued into 1861. But the crisis was kept under control and the border state never joined the seceding states.

WAR -- THE BEGINNING

Rebel guns fired at the federal installation at Fort Sumter, South Carolina, on April 12, 1861. A few days later, President Abraham Lincoln called for 75,000 volunteers to quell the rebellion. The event triggered neighbors to act on their convictions. Some families declared their loyalty to the blue, others to the gray, and men from Olney and the surrounding villages began the fight for their cause -- the Union or the Confederacy.

Following President Lincoln's call for volunteers, Governor Thomas Hicks decreed that Maryland troops would only be dispatched for protection of the nation's capital. Because Maryland was so close to Washington, Federal troops had already occupied Rockville and other areas of the state by June to protect the capital against attack. Outspoken advocates of secession were arrested on the streets as were the citizens suspected of spying or encouraging desertion to the Confederacy. Federal troops often intimidated voters.

Montgomery County served as a thoroughfare for the armies of both sides. Federal troops marched on county roads toward Washington to protect the capital or came through on the way to engagements in southern states. Confederate troops moved through to engagements in Pennsylvania or crossed the Potomac into the county trying to seize Washington from the north. Supplies for Union troops were hauled to Georgetown, a major port, before they were distributed to the troops.

Even though no great battles were fought here, the war caused deep psychological wounds. Residents were unsure of what to expect from troops of either side. The sounds of gun-firing and cannonading from battles at Monocacy, Antietam, and even Gettysburg sent chills of anxiety through Olney farmers as they plowed their fields. Anxiety turned to fear when residents saw thousands of strangers marching through the streets of their small towns and firing at each other. Fencing was stolen and found its way into campfires. Pigs and chickens disappeared wherever soldiers from either side camped.

Troops showed little loyalty to citizens who sympathized with their cause, and neither side protected its supporters. Union soldiers robbed Union sympathizers as well as Southern sympathizers. Confederate troops did the same. Troops passing through took whatever they wanted or needed, often committed acts of vandalism, and when it was convenient, made the county their campground. They skirmished with each other, harassed residents, stole food and supplies, and raided the farmers for fresh horses.

Although citizens were not taken prisoner, Union and Confederate officers took them captive as guides before they were released. When traveling, citizens had to get a pass from the armies so they would not be detained. Villagers also feared the roaming troops and hid their belongings from both the Union and Confederate armies.

The split in loyalties between neighbors began early in the war and often pitted old-time friends against each other. Within days following President Lincoln's call for volunteers, the Sixth Massachusetts Regiment and several Pennsylvania militia units reached Baltimore. Ridgely Brown of Sunshine and Thomas Griffith of Olney, set out to lead a group of volunteers to defend Baltimore, and flew the Confederate flag as they traveled. They stopped at Brookeville where word was that troops from the north were on their way toward Washington. At Baltimore, a crowd began rioting. Soldiers and civilians were killed, and the tragedy of war began -- tallying the first casualties.

Less than two months after President Lincoln called for volunteers to suppress the rebellion at Fort Sumter, Brown enlisted in the First Virginia Calvary to fight for the Confederate cause. When he earned the rank of second lieutenant, he formed the First Maryland Cavalry. As a major and lieutenant colonel, Brown commanded the First Maryland in the Shenandoah Valley, West Virginia, and at Gettysburg. His calvary was credited with saving Richmond from capture by Union troops.

Brown, a Confederate hero, was killed in 1864 in a skirmish. After the war his body was buried in the family cemetery at his homestead, Elton, about six miles north of Olney. A bronze memorial plaque on a wall in St. John's Episcopal Church in Olney memorializes Brown's dedication to the Confederate cause. The inscription reads he "died June 1, 1864 after being mortally wounded that day in a victorious charge near Ashland, Virginia."

When the war ended a local branch of the United Confederate Veterans and a chapter of the United Daughters of the Confederacy were named in Brown's honor. An historic marker that pays tribute to Brown is located on Route 97, Georgia Avenue, just north of the intersection of Route 650.

Thomas Griffith II was another local resident who fought with distinction for the Confederacy. Born and raised at Edgehill near Unity about 15 miles northwest of Olney, Griffith came from a well-known family, a descendent of Colonel Henry Griffith II, a patriot who served with distinction in the American Revolution. Thomas followed in the family tradition, and served as Captain of the First Maryland Cavalry of the Confederate Army. The house in which he lived in Olney still stands on Route 108 about 1- 1/2 miles west of the Georgia Avenue/Route 108 intersection.

Griffith lived to the ripe old age of 81 and died on July 12, 1912. The current resident of Griffith's Olney house recalled that farmers in the area fought for the Confederate army including his grandfather's brother and all his first cousins. "I was eight when grandmother died, and she was 15 when the Civil War broke out," the resident said. "She remembered various armies coming through the area and her father and the other men would take the horses down in the woods and tie them to trees to try to hide them." Silver and other valuables were buried, he said, to protect the belongings from the troops as they came through.

Many local farmers fought in the Union army too. But none achieved the status of heros of their cause like Brown and Griffith in the Confederate calvary.

FEAR AT HOME

Olney became the local center for news about the war. The village was a natural gathering place for residents who came to town to get wagon wheels fixed or to purchase supplies at the stores. The shop owners were probably eager to pass on any snippet of news they had about the war, even though the news may have been old or inaccurate.

The crossroads became even more important after the Federal Government ordered a military road be established that passed through Olney. Author Martha C. Nesbitt wrote about the road in *Chronicles of Sandy Spring Friends Meeting and Environs* (1987). "Additional military traffic coursed through the heart of the Sandy Spring neighborhood, following the Federal Government's order to establish a military road between Laurel (strategically located on the Baltimore & Ohio Railroad), and General Nathaniel P. Bank's headquarters at Darnestown." The route went from Laurel, through Ashton, Sandy Spring, Olney, Rockville and into Darnestown.

Both Confederate and Federal troops occupied the village at different times as they passed through on their campaigns elsewhere. Often they arrived via the 'pike' as Georgia Avenue was called. The military traffic produced numerous encounters between soldiers and citizens. Although no battles were fought here, Charles F. Brooke, a descendant of one of the earliest settlers, recalled a skirmish in Olney that involved his father, and spoke about it in 1926 when he delivered a speech to the Men's Club at St. John's Church.

"I can distinctly remember bullet holes in a building which was built on the site of the old pottery, which came there by reason of a lively skirmish during the Civil War," Brooke said. The approximate spot where the pottery stood was on the northeast corner of today's intersection.

Brooke said his father, George Brooke who lived at Brooke Grove about two miles east of the intersection, was en route to Olney for news of the war. George stopped at the home of his sister, Sarah Brooke Farquhar, who was living at the Olney House. As he approached, she came running from the house yelling, "Why George, the town is full of Rebels!" Determined to

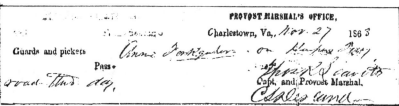

Figure 1   A pass from Union troops, which was "good this day," was issued to Anna Farquhar on November 27, 1863 to travel from Charlestown, Virginia, to Harpers Ferry. Courtesy of the Sandy Spring Museum.

protect his horse George replied, "I'll make old Charley take me home once more." As he turned back toward home he noticed two Confederate soldiers starting toward him. George got home safely but was afraid the troops would follow him to take his horses, and told the field hands to quickly hide the animals.

"About the time of his reaching home, we heard firing at the village," recalled Charles, "and he [Dad] went back at once to find the village in possession of Federal troops, who had captured one of the Confederates on the road above St. John's Church. This man had but one arm and was riding with his bridle reins in his teeth and shooting back with his revolver. In bringing his pistol forward to cock it, he shot his own horse in the head and was captured."

Other recollections of life in the area during the war were penned by Mary Coffin Brooke. She taught at Fair Hill Boarding School which had been established at the old Richard Brooke homestead many years earlier. Brooke taught at Fair Hill for 11 years, from 1854 through 1865 when the school was sold.

In *Memories of Eighty Years* (1916) Brooke wrote of her experience as a teacher during that traumatic period. "In 1861, when the Civil War came on," Brooke wrote, "the excitement that existed throughout the country could not be kept out of the school. Girls from the North and the South (not all of whom were Quakers), were so divided in sentiment that the only way to preserve peace and harmony was to forbid all discussion of the war." When Southern sympathizers withdrew their daughters from the school, attendance quickly dropped from 40 to 14.

The sounds of gunfire carried for miles and the responsibility to calm and reassure her students weighed heavy upon Brooke. Recalling the tense and strained period Brooke wrote, "Fair Hill was an old house and often the cannonading on the upper Potomac, or even firing in platoons in practice, would rattle the windows with a suddenness that was a little hard on one's nerves, especially as it was necessary to maintain an appearance of composure. I learned to carry a non-committal face, and to go on as if armies were not marching and counter-marching up and down the land."

Describing the anxiety and fear provoked by nearby fighting and perennial marching troops Brooke wrote, "My sleeping room was at the head of the steps that led up from the front hall, which was never lighted, and, as tales of deserters and guerrillas were always afloat, I never undressed at night until I was satisfied that my room had no stray occupants."

Even though some religious groups did not believe in participating in war, allegiance to the country was in evidence. Explaining the reaction of the local Quaker community Brooke noted, "The Friends are not a fighting people, but Sandy Spring proved her loyalty in many ways. Not only were war taxes cheerfully paid, but in the early days of the conflict, before hospitals were established, the sick and wounded near us were supplied with suitable clothing and food."

Brooke's memories included the evening when General Joseph Hooker's brigade of Union soldiers camped at Fair Hill. "At Fair Hill, they commandeered the four-horse team and big farm wagon, and, in one night, burned the new rails around an eighty-acre field where they encamped, but I believe that the government eventually made some return." As the troops were on their way back to Rockville, Brooke noted that the soldiers stuffed their knapsacks with potatoes from a nearby farm, Willow Grove, located off Batchellors Forest Road.

UNION TROOPS IN THE VILLAGE

In early September 1862, the Confederate Army crossed the Potomac into western Montgomery County around White's Ford, a favorite crossing point between Maryland and Virginia. Recognizing the threat to the capital, Union troops moved out from Washington to provide a barrier of protection from the advancing southerners. Other Union soldiers moved toward the northwest in search of Confederates, and those troop movements later resulted in the battles of South Mountain and Antietam. The First Corps and the Ninth Corps, the right wing of General George B. McClellan's army under General Ambrose Burnside, marched out the 'pike,' Georgia Avenue, North. They passed through Olney and Brookeville on September 8 and 9, 1862.

In *Old Homes and History of Montgomery County, Maryland* (1981) Roger Brooke Farquhar wrote about his grandmother's and father's experiences with the Union generals that September. "On one occasion General Hooker had dinner with Mrs. (Sarah Brooke) Farquhar in her home, and she reported him to be courteous and gentlemanly. On another day, her son Roger rode horseback along with General McClellan from Norbeck to Olney and wrote in his diary that McClellan was 'a fine looking man'."

The opposing armies eventually clashed in the battle of Antietam at Sharpsburg. Both the Confederate and Union forces suffered heavy losses, and Lee withdrew his troops from northern territory and retreated to Virginia.

CONFEDERATES IN TOWN

Olney remained fairly quiet until June 28, 1863. In *Civil War Guide to Montgomery County, MD* (1983) author Charles T. Jacobs wrote that three brigades of General J.E.B. Stuart's Confederate Cavalry Corps swept through Montgomery County on a daring raid, and, "moved through [Olney] encumbered by the 150 Union wagons captured earlier that day...."

The supply wagons were captured in Rockville where the corps took several hundred prisoners including pro-Union sympathizers and Federal soldiers. Noting the mixed sentiment of county residents Jacobs wrote that at Rockville the Rebel troop "received a mixed reception -- the southern leaning citizens enthusiastic while the pro-Unionists sought hiding places throughout the town."

Stuart's troops headed toward Gettysburg via Old Baltimore Road and the Brookeville Turnpike, Georgia Avenue. As they passed through Olney, Stuart's troops captured as many fresh horses as they could find from the farms.

In Volume I of *The Annals of Sandy Spring*, historian William H. Farquhar recorded the 1863 incident as the first neighborhood contact with Rebel forces.

> In the first summer month, the quiet of the neighborhood began to be disturbed by rumors of hostile invasion. The month had nearly passed, and our anxieties on this account were nearly abated, when a serene Sabbath evening, the 28th of June, brought us unexpectedly our unwelcome visitors. A small troop of cavalry, wearing the gray uniform which we had hitherto only read of, or else had seen under circumstances that rendered its wearer powerless to injure quitting the large body of 4,000, under the famous "Mr. Steward," actually defiled along the roads leading through the centre of this our own neighborhood. At first we saw them with most incredulous eyes: it was a sight long to be remembered -- our first actual contact with the terrible Rebellion. Yet after(especially to us who lost no horses) it was a mere ripple of the mighty wave.

Another Farquhar, Roger B. made the following comments in his diary: "1863 -- Rebel army under Stewart[sic] went by Olney. Took my horse 'Mike,' three of mother's horses and eight from Uncle George's (Brooke Grove) and from most everyone in the neighborhood. Force estimated from 8,000 to 10,000. Came thru Poolesville and Rockville and captured 150 U.S. wagons, with mules, and quantity of stores."

In his Civil War guide Charles Jacobs wrote about an incident during the 1863 passage that describes the conflict in allegiance among residents during the war. "A local resident...returning from church in Mechanicsville (Olney) to his home (the site of the present Manor Country Club), reported being stopped by Rebel pickets on the Brookeville Turnpike and engaging in a conversation with General Stuart himself before being allowed to complete his journey home." Jacobs said that the next day the resident gave maps of the area to a Union colonel who was pursuing the rebels.

Leaving Olney, Stuart's Cavalry Corps stopped in Brookeville long enough to release the majority of their prisoners and take horses from nearby farms. But they had been encumbered by the wagons and prisoners they captured at Rockville, and Stuart's troops did not arrive at Gettysburg until July 2, the second day of the three-day battle. The Confederates were defeated the following day and some historians believe that the delayed arrival of Stuart's troops to assist General Lee's Army may have influenced the outcome of the war.

The Annals mention the noises from the Gettysburg battle that must have prompted a good deal of anxiety. Referring to the sounds of war the record reads, "the sound of cannonading had been plainly heard in Sandy Spring, fifty air-miles away."

Following the Gettysburg battle, soldiers trooped through the area again on their way to Washington, and historical notes indicate that at least one soldier made a return visit. Lieutenant George E. Tilley, a Union officer, came through Sandy Spring in the fall of 1915 on his way to a reunion in Washington. He wanted to revisit the farm of Richard T. Bentley at Bloomfield where he and his fellow Federal troops had camped on their way from Gettysburg back to Washington in July, 1863. Bentley had also operated the Sandy Spring store during the war. When Tilley returned to his home in New York, he wrote a letter recalling his war experience and spoke of the hospitality of the Sandy Spring community that greeted soldiers who passed through.

The Annals quoted the letter that read, "The recollection of that depleted country store...has remained as vivid in my mind as any incident of my army life, and the very genial and benevolent face of the grand proprietor will never be forgotten. He served us a royal feast on that early morning, when almost famished from want of food on a long march, we were still within one day of our old camp in Washington."

CONFEDERATES AGAIN

In July 1864, villagers of Olney and Sandy Spring heard the sound of cannon in battle once again. Confederate forces marched into Maryland and faced Union troops along the Monocacy in

Frederick County. In the Annals Farquhar wrote: "On the 9th of that month occurred the engagement at Monocacy; and the same evening came the news, 'the Rebels hold Frederick and the line of the Monocacy'...In the evening we learn from Charles H. Brooke, who had been for awhile their captive, that they are in or near Laytonsville." At the time, Brooke lived at Falling Green, a farmhouse still standing on the north side of Route 108, just west of the Olney Mill community.

News traveled quickly about the battles in the county and William H. Farquhar noted, "The next news came, 'the Rebels are at Stanmore,' whence they soon departed but not empty-handed." Stanmore was the home of Francis and Caroline Hallowell Miller who were operating a private boarding school in their home. Stanmore, which no longer stands, was located on Route 108. While the Rebels were at Olney, Francis was held captive for a time.

During that same invasion, Benjamin Hallowell, the highly respected lecturer and educator who lived at his farmhouse Rockland on Route 108 also did not get through the war unscathed. His experiences led him to mourn the loss of his long-time faithful horse, Ande, and grieve for his former students who served in the Confederate and Union armies.

Hallowell described the invasion of Olney by Confederate troops in *Autobiography of Benjamin Hallowell* (1883). "In the summer of 1864 a Confederate officer, accompanied by two soldiers galloped up the lawn at Rockland and finding my riding-horse fastened in front of the house, they loosed her and took her off before I could get to them." The soldiers stopped at the barn and Hallowell wrote that he ran and grabbed onto his beloved horse, Ande, and held the bridle rein. Hallowell explained that the officer, "then presented a pistol to my breast, and said he would shoot me if I did not let go. I looked him firmly in the face, and told him I could not do it; the horse was mine; the Confederate soldiers had taken our three best horses the previous year, and this was the only one I had left, and I could not, spare her." The officers left. "I was closely observant of his countenance," Hallowell continued, "and of the muscles of the finger that rested on the trigger."

The next morning Hallowell rode Ande over to see his sister-in-law, Sarah B. Farquhar who was residing at Olney House, and met a Confederate officer and two soldiers who demanded his horse. After Hallowell refused, the officer took him to his general who ordered the officer to, "Take that horse." When Hallowell refused to comply, the officer asked him if he was far from home. Hallowell replied that he was not. "Then you can readily walk there?" the officer asked. Hallowell replied that he could. "He came up to my saddle, cooley and deliberately unbuckled the girth," Hallowell wrote, "took hold of the saddle with one hand in front and the other behind me and pulled it and me over (I resting on his shoulder), and laid me down at full length as gently as if I had been an infant." Hallowell said he had no feeling of "unkindness" about the war years, but "they took nine of our very best horses (they being excellent judges, and taking none but the best)."

In earlier years, Hallowell had founded and administered a private academy in Alexandria, Virginia. In his autobiography Hallowell expressed his sadness that his former students were fighting against each other in the pursuit of their causes. "In the year 1860," he wrote, "seeing that a great sectional strife was approaching, in which my former students, who felt to me almost like my own children, were arrayed on opposite sides...I determined, as far as practicable, to keep my mind and feelings from all participation in it." Hallowell kept from reading or making inquiries about the war from 1860 through 1863.

Hallowell described his feelings about the success of his most famous student, Robert E. Lee. "Although General Lee had been one of my students, in great favor, and a warm personal friendship had existed between us from that time, so that it would seem natural that my sympathies should be all with him and his success, yet when I heard that General Meade had arrested his progress and driven him across the Potomac to his own State, my heart rejoiced!"

A WIDOW'S DECEPTION

There are few accounts about women's activities during the Civil War. Fortunately, there is a story about an astute widow who matched wits and fooled the Confederate soldiers who came to take her horses.

Elizabeth Kirk had run Woodburn, a farm on Batchellors Forest Road, since the death of her husband Mahlon in 1860. In *Old Homes and History of Montgomery County,* Roger Brooke Farquhar recounted the story of Kirk's courage and her wisely planned encounter with troops who were looking for some fresh horses.

> "...one afternoon a platoon of Confederate soldiers came to the farm, intending to make off with all the horses. She knew they had stripped many of the other farms of suitable cavalry mounts. Widow Kirk met the men with disarming courtesy, inviting them into the house to have something to eat. While giving them a real treat, she 'tipped off' her men, and the horses were soon hidden in the deep pine woods safe from discovery. The soldiers, their hunger well satisfied, found only one old plow horse in its stall and galloped away."

THE WAR YEARS

Without a doubt, horses were among the top priorities of both Union and Confederate troops. Without a doubt, the farmers of Olney and surrounding communities suffered economically because of the loss of their best horses. But the trauma of the Civil War to citizens in small farming villages can only be experienced by trying to imagine what it must have been like -- hearing the sounds of booming cannons, watching the marching troops, seeing the skirmishes in the streets, fearing the soldiers who were camped on the farms and scrambling to hide the family valuables, food, and horses.

Without a doubt, the experience left emotional scars, and those scars took years to heal.

Chapter 6

CULTIVATING THE MIND AND SOUL

Education and religion, the seeds that cultivate the mind and the soul, were deeply woven into the lives of the colonists. In their churches and schools the early settlers found the guidance and hope that nourished their growth and the growth of the Olney farming community.

In the early years, when Montgomery County had no public schools, education was a private and often a religious concern. Several of the first private day and boarding schools were founded by the churches.

PRIVATE SCHOOLS

Since the county's public school system was not firmly established until the late 1800s, wealthier families sent their children to private academies or hired tutors. The Sandy Spring Quaker Community founded several school and provided the vision that led the way toward a public school system in the Olney area.

FAIR HILL

Fair Hill was Olney's first private school, founded by the Baltimore Yearly Meeting of Friends in 1820 in the former home of Colonel Richard Brooke. Benjamin Hallowell (1799-1877), a young Quaker from Pennsylvania, came to Mechanicsville to teach that year.

"Roxbury" Samuel Thomas and his wife, Anna had searched for someone to teach mathematics at the new school and to assist them. But it seems they let Hallowell figure out how to make the journey from Pennsylvania to Fair Hill.

"On arriving at Baltimore I went to Issac Tyson's to inquire how I should get to Fair Hill," he wrote in the *Autobiography of Benjamin Hallowell* (1884). "'Why,' said he, 'there is no way; it is

the most out-of-the-way place in the world.' I felt much dis-
couraged which perhaps he perceived."

 Hallowell's all-day journey to Fair Hill began with a stagecoach
ride from Baltimore to Laurel. When he arrived, Hallowell inquired about his destination and discovered there was no "public
conveyance" to Mechanicsville. But a farmer provided a horse,
cart and driver to carry the trunk. Hallowell walked. In describing
his transportation Hallowell wrote that the young driver had, "but
one line to his horse, and it was truly a very poor and unsightly
outfit." After getting lost and trying to guide the young boy
through woods and over streams in this "get-up," Hallowell finally
arrived at Fair Hill about 10 o'clock in the evening, just in time
to retire.

Hallowell remained at Fair Hill until 1821 when he decided to,
"...look for a home elsewhere." He enjoyed his stay there, describ-

PHOTO 8 Fair Hill as it looked in 1975. The former Richard Brooke home served
as a school from 1820 to 1865 and then became a private residence. The building,
which burned in the late 1970s, was located where the Olney Village Mart
shopping center is today. Photo courtesy of the Park Historian's office,
Maryland-National Capital Park and Planning Commission.

ing it as, "the happy condition of things at Fair Hill." But one incident particularly impressed the young man.

In his book Hallowell explained that in a gleeful fervor, the young male students had dug a deep hole. An old sow had fallen into it, and the boys frantically ran to the superintendent for help. The superintendent quickly assessed the situation -- a several hundred pound animal in a deep hole -- and said, "Now, boys, you have dug a grave for the old beast, now bury her." The boys liked this "gruesome" game and enthusiastically began filling the hole with the earth using spades and paddles, and anything else they could find to do the job. They even used their feet to quickly push the earth to fill up the hole. But the old beast would not stay buried. As earth was pushed into the hole, she would rise above it. When the grave was full, Hallowell wrote, she quietly walked out.

"This was all play to them," Hallowell said. "Had he [the superintendent] ordered them to fill up the hole they had dug, in order that she might get out, this would have been work, and it would have been a long time in all probability, before it was accomplished." Summing up the instruction from that incident Hallowell wrote, "Everything can be moved if we touch the right spring."

After teaching at Fair Hill and other private facilities, Hallowell felt his training, "was admirably adapted to form my character," and decided to establish his own school. He took his family to Alexandria and in 1824 founded a private academy for boys. The school was very successful and operated for almost 40 years. One of his most famous pupils was Robert E. Lee, the future general who would later lead the Confederacy during the Civil War. While attending the academy Lee was preparing for West Point, and Hallowell tutored him in mathematics.

Hallowell left his mark on Alexandria society. He founded a water company and made some notable contributions to the practice of agriculture. In 1834 Hallowell was one of several residents that established a lyceum in Alexandria to hold lectures and debates.

Elected the first president Hallowell wrote, "I delivered the first lecture, which was on Vegetable Physiology. It was the commencement of my attention being turned to that very interesting subject." Well known for his talents as a mathematician, astronomer and scientist, Hallowell was in constant demand as a speaker. In 1854 he delivered lectures on astronomy at the Smithsonian Institution. Hallowell remained president of the Lyceum until 1842 when his two young nephews took over the academy. Then he returned to Rockland in Mechanicsville to farm. But Hallowell went back to the academy for several years when his nephews no longer wanted to continue as schoolmasters. His reputation as a stern taskmaster must have followed him when he came back to Olney. Local historians say students at the academy referred to it in private as "Brimstone Academy."

As Hallowell was making his reputation in Alexandria, Fair Hill Academy in Mechanicsville struggled to remain open. Roxbury Samuel Thomas and his wife Anna had died a few years after opening the academy. On May 5, 1851, Richard and Mary Kirk reopened Fair Hill Boarding School to serve girls. The school remained in operation until 1865.

The school year began on October 1st and continued until the end of June. Tuition for the nine-month program cost $140. A circular describing the school reads, "the design of this Institution is to impart a full and thorough knowledge of the various branches of a solid and useful education." Students of today would be surprised to learn that in addition to reading, writing, arithmetic, spelling, and composition, private-school students of the mid-1800s were taught natural and moral philosophy, chemistry, mythology, physiology, botany, algebra and geometry, and the French, German and Latin languages. At the end of each six-week period the students received "character papers" that described their progress.

In 1854 Mary Coffin Brooke accepted a teaching post at Fair Hill, and she remained there for 11 years. In *Memories of Eighty Years* (1916) Brooke described her students as eager and conscientious.

FAIR HILL BOARDING SCHOOL,

FOR GIRLS.

Sandy Spring, Montgomery County, Md.

The Fair Hill Farm and Property having been leased by the Baltimore Yearly Meeting of Friends to Richard S. Kirk for the purposes of a Girls' School, the Institution was opened for the reception of Scholars on the 5th day of the 5th month, 1851 ; and it has been in successful operation since that period, with an average class of about forty boarders, each successive term.

This Institution is situated 18 miles north of Washington, and 28 miles southwest of Baltimore ; and the cars leaving the former place at 8½ o'clock a. m., and the latter at 9 o'clock a. m., connect with a *daily stage* at Laurel, thus furnishing a direct communication with the School, distant 14 miles.

The neighborhood is noted for its healthfulness, intelligence, and morality. The situation of the School is pleasant and elevated, commanding a fine prospect ; and the Buildings, which have been recently repaired and enlarged, are well adapted to the purposes of a Boarding School.

Course of Study.

The design of this Institution is to impart a full and thorough knowledge of the various branches of a solid and useful Education. The studies *actually* pursued are :

Spelling, Reading, Writing, Drawing, Geography, Grammar, Composition, Arithmetic, Book-keeping, Natural and Moral Philosophy, Physical Geography, Chemistry, Mythology, Physiology, Botany Geology, History, Algebra, Geometry, and the French, German, and Latin Languages.

Figure 1   This is a page from the circular of Fair Hill Boarding School in 1862. Courtesy of the Sandy Spring Museum.

But the conditions under which the young scholars studied, Brooke wrote, were less than ideal.

"Our choice of light for the schoolroom was limited to candles, lard oil lamps, and benzine lamps," she noted. "Of course benzine gave the best light, but was too unsafe. I was not willing to have one of the last named lamps on my own desk, for the responsibility of other people's children is a grave one." Teachers gave one small lard lamp to every three or four girls to share, and she said, "...as they used slates for their examples, I don't see why their eyes were not ruined."

Brooke was excited when oil lamps finally became available. "But the happy day came," she wrote, "when coal oil was discovered, and a refined and quite expensive oil was put on the market. The proprietor of the school at once procured it, and four large suspended lamps almost made daylight. I felt as if the millennium had come."

The Civil War changed school life. Attendance dropped and by the end of the war Fair Hill was no longer a viable operation. The Baltimore Yearly Meeting of Friends sold the building and grounds in 1865. However there were other private schools in Olney.

STANMORE

When Benjamin Hallowell finally retired from teaching, he wanted to concentrate his energy on farming. But his devotion to education never waned. In 1858 Hallowell gave his nephew Francis Miller 30 acres of his Rockland farm to build a house and to open a country boarding school for boys. Miller built the school, Stanmore, across from today's Olney Theater on Route 108. Stanmore operated as a boys school until 1867.

That same year Stanmore became a girls' school. Caroline Hallowell Miller, Francis' wife and Benjamin's daughter, served as principal while Francis decided to pursue a legal education. A circular about Stanmore dated May 1869 reads, "Lectures will be delivered, weekly, by William Henry Farquhar and Henry C. Hallowell, on Natural Science, Intellectual Philosophy, History, and General Literature, accompanied by such illustrations as are calculated to impress upon the minds of the pupils the principles to which their attention is invited." The circular noted that health permitting, Caroline's father, Benjamin, would deliver lectures on astronomy, geology and vegetable physiology.

Mary Coffin Brooke taught at Stanmore four years. Young girls came from across the country to attend. Historic accounts indicate a niece of Ulysses S. Grant (U.S. President 1869-1877) attended the school. The president occasionally drove out to Olney to pick up the young lady for a weekend at the White House. Stanmore remained a boarding school for girls until it closed in 1878.

ROCKLAND

Following the closing of Stanmore Henry C. Hallowell, Benjamin's son, and his wife Sarah opened the Rockland homestead of his late father as a school for girls. Records indicate students came from 12 states, including New York and California, and the island of Bermuda to attend.

A circular about the Rockland School for Girls reads "This Institution is designed to be a select school, in which girls can obtain a thorough education under judicious and careful superintendence," and, "It is one of the most healthy locations in the country, and in the midst of a community noted for its intelligence, industry and morality." Rockland served young ladies from across the country until 1892.

Today the Rockland farm has been subdivided, and hundreds of homes and streets replace the wheat and corn crops. The house is on a street named Brimstone Academy Road. Whoever named the street must not have realized that Hallowell's academy was not really named "Brimstone."

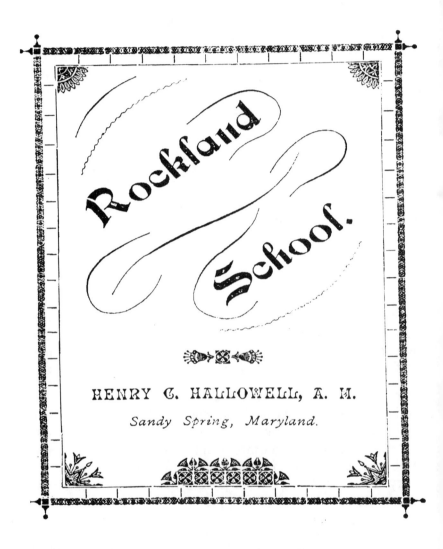

Figure 2 Title page of the circular for Rockland School in 1886. Henry C. Hallowell used the same format for the circular for several years. Courtesy of Sandy Spring Museum.

ROCKLAND SCHOOL
FOR GIRLS,
SANDY SPRING, MARYLAND.

This Institution is designed to be a SELECT SCHOOL in which Girls can obtain a thorough education under judicious and careful superintendence.

The Proprietor and Principal is a graduate of Yale College, and was associated with his father, Benjamin Hallowell, in the Alexandria Boarding School.

The Buildings are well arranged for the comfort and health of the Scholars. They are situated in SANDY SPRING neighborhood, Montgomery County, Maryland, about eighteen miles north of Washington City, and twenty-eight miles from Baltimore.

It is one of the most healthy locations in the country, and in the midst of a community noted for its intelligence, industry and morality.

The next school year will commence September 19th, 1887, and end June 15th, 1888.

ACCESS.

The school is easily accessible from Baltimore or Washington.

1. A morning stage runs daily from Laurel Station, on the Washington Branch of the Baltimore and Ohio Rail Road, passing by the door.

Figure 3 First page of the circular for Rockland School. Courtesy of the Sandy Spring Museum.

PUBLIC SCHOOLS

While Montgomery County enjoys an excellent reputation for its commitment to public education today, that was not always the case. Public school education in the early 1800s suffered in comparison with private education. "Not much attention was given to popular education, or, more properly speaking, public-school education, in the early history of Maryland," wrote J. Thomas Scharf in *History of Western Maryland* (1882).

In early Maryland history, providing an education for children rated a very low priority and for a good reason. The colonists were busy settling a country -- chopping down trees, clearing and plowing fields, butchering and preparing meat for winter and fighting unforseen hazards and hardships.

"They were peculiarly self-dependent," wrote Scharf "and could not be taught the advantages to be derived...from the expenditure of their hard-earned substance for the education of those who were bound to them by no tie..."

Guy Jewell provides an account of early attempts at education in Maryland in *From One Room to Open Space, A History of Montgomery County Schools from 1732 to 1965* (1976). Jewell notes that public schools had a, "hard, slow beginning," here as they did in the rest of Maryland. "It surprises Marylanders to be reminded that in 1860 there were 33 states in the Union; but only two, Maryland and South Carolina, lacked a statewide public school system," he wrote.

Early attempts to establish a public school system in Maryland began in 1812 when the General Assembly passed the Bank Road Bill. Companies that wanted to build toll roads and offer banking benefits were assessed a fee. The fee went into an educational fund for poor children. However Montgomery County did very little about public education and by 1819 had not collected its share of the educational fund.

Some headway in education was made in 1839 when a special act was passed to establish primary schools in the county. A manager was appointed for each district and schools were established in some areas. But, "Montgomery County's commitment to education remained haphazard until 1860," wrote Richard K. MacMaster and Ray Eldon Hiebert in *A Grateful Remembrance* (1976).

The educational climate in the state improved when the General Assembly established a public school system for Montgomery County. A Board of Commissioners of Public Schools was authorized to employ teachers, develop study courses, and maintain schoolhouses. It is not surprising that the first school board president was William H. Farquhar, a Sandy Spring Quaker who had served as principal of Fair Hill Academy.

FIRST PUBLIC SCHOOL

The first public school in Olney dates back to about 1875, when the school board bought a lot adjacent to St. John's Episcopal Church on Route 108 for $175. The one-room school house, a 24-by 30-foot structure, was built for $575. A local resident who attended the school around 1920 described it as, "a single room with an iron stove in the middle... four or five feet high. Part of the teachers' job was to carry the coal to the stove...there were no indoor bathrooms" he said. Outhouses were located behind St. John's Church.

The resident also recalled that when he attended the one-room school, only 20 to 25 kids attended class. Because Olney was a farming community and the children lived on farms, They stayed home from school to help with farm work at harvest time.

Another resident remembered that Boy Scout meetings were held in the school building around 1933 to 1935. He described the school as a frame building with a pot-bellied stove. About 60 years later the building was sold for $1,000, and was eventually torn down.

PHOTO 9 Students at the first public school in Olney take time for recess, always a popular activity. The one-room frame building was constructed about 1875 and was located on Route 108, just west of the Olney intersection. The building was demolished in the 1930s. Photo courtesy of the Sandy Spring Museum.

SHERWOOD HIGH SCHOOL

In 1883 Mrs. Mary Roberts donated land opposite her home, "Sherwood," for a small, private Friends' school. Sherwood Academy was built and maintained by the Quaker community for several years.

The school population grew. In March 1906, the owners of the academy, the Board of Directors of the Friends Central School Association, offered the school to the county under the Public School Laws of the State of Maryland. The association proposed certain terms in the offer to the state. They asked the school commissioners to improve the property by erecting a building for

150 pupils, to complete the building by the fall school term of 1910, and to use the property for a high school.

The building that was already on the site was donated to the state, and the county assumed its management. Sherwood became a public school in September 1906. But the General Assembly had to pass legislation, the "Donation Act of 1908," before the county could accept the Friends' offer.

Construction of a two-story building began in 1909. The old frame building became the assembly hall, and in 1910 the school opened for a new term, even though the building was not yet completed. Classes were scattered around the area until work on the building was finished.

PHOTO 10 Sherwood High School as it looked in 1915. A larger building replaced this structure in the 1950s. Photo courtesy of the Sandy Spring Museum.

Since farming was such a strong livelihood, classes reflected the needs of the community, and Sherwood High School included agricultural classes. Boys performed agricultural experiments as part of their school work. Over time Sherwood served grades 1-11. A resident who attended in 1922 said several grades shared each room.

During the early years students walked or rode in a horse-drawn buggy. Children who came by horse rented space at a shed on the school property. When it snowed, students rode to school in a horse-drawn sleigh. The first school bus system to serve Sherwood started in the fall of 1923. Two private automobiles were used--a Dodge touring car driven by a student from Spencerville and a Model T Ford driven by a student from Brighton. Each driver picked up four or five students. The students' parents and the county split the cost, each paying $2.50 per student.

The bell in front of the present school has a history of its own. It came from Triadelphia, a nearby town that had been destroyed by a flood in 1889.

In 1902, Alice Farquhar, principal of Sherwood School visited Triadelphia, a town north of Brookeville. She inquired about a bell that had been purchased by Triadelphia Montgomery Mill Company, a business that had been in the town. In the town's heyday, the bell had called the mill hands to work, but since the flood, the bell had not been used. Farquhar raised $50 and bought the bell for Sherwood School. For the next 50 years it was rung to call students to their work. In 1950 the school system built the present high school building which modernized in 1991. The bell is now enclosed in a small stone structure outside the school.

SPIRITUAL MATTERS

Lord Baltimore, founder of the Maryland Colony, was intent on protecting religious freedom for the colonists. To preserve freedom the colony passed the Act of Religious Toleration in 1649. The act guaranteed that "no person or persons whatsoever within this province...professing to believe in Jesus Christ shall henceforth be anyways troubled, molested or discountenanced for or in respect of his or her religion."

But in 1692, the Church of England became the official church of the Maryland province. Catholics were prohibited from holding public office and religious services. Because Catholic churches could not be erected, many Catholics set aside a room in their house for worship. Marylanders were heavily taxed to support the established Church.

Like the Catholic community, Quakers too were penalized and denied their civil liberties. However Quakers could not hold office because they would not take the oath to the king. The general assembly in the mid-1600s had allowed the quakers "to promise," not swear, allegiance to the government. Eventually the Quakers regained the rights they had been denied.

When the early Quaker settlers came to the area in the 1700s, they continued their ties to religion. Like other members of other denominations they met in each others' homes until there were enough families to build a meeting house.

During that time neighbors were distanced by acres of farmland, so the church provided the only educational nurturing and social life outside the home. Church was a place where neighbors had a chance to talk with each other before and after services or while attending events. The church also offered spiritual support in times of hardship. Religious ties were strong and it was not unusual for a church member to donate land for a new house of worship or a graveyard.

Strong religious and social ties continued into the 20th century. One long-time resident remarked that the church provided the only social life available for many residents during the early- to mid- 1900s. Churches held several yearly events, and families contributed time to church projects, perhaps as a welcome break from their farming duties. Churches held a number of fund raisers including dinners, Christmas bazaars, and antique shows. They also raised money for less fortunate residents.

ST. PETER'S CATHOLIC CHURCH

St. Peter's Catholic Church of Olney began as a mission at Hawling's River in the early 1800s. In the beginning the parish was so small there was no pastor to serve the congregation. The pastor of St. Mary's in Rockville came to celebrate the Eucharist for parishioners on the fifth Sunday of the month wherever the congregation met.

In 1860 shortly before the Civil War, the first St. Peter's Church was built at Mt. Zion between Olney and Laytonsville on land donated by the Watkins family. Father John Doughery together with the help of parishioners built a clapboard chapel with four windows and a large cross above the altar. The church seated about 25 people.

Following the Civil War the population of Olney grew, and the small church no longer accommodated the congregation. In 1897 the pastor of St. Mary's purchased a tract of land on the east side of Georgia Avenue, just south of the intersection of Routes 108 and 97. A chapel was built with a main and side altar, two sacristies, a choir loft, 10 stained glass windows and seating for 100 parishioners. The church was dedicated in 1898.

St. Peter's remained a mission until 1953 when a resident pastor was appointed. The chapel served the Catholic community until 1957. A parish hall and school were built on Route 108 in 1957, and today the old chapel exists only in pictures. On Sunday, June 18, 1987, ground breaking ceremonies for a new church on the Route 108 site took place. The cornerstone of the church was dedicated on December 17, 1988 at a noon mass.

ST. JOHN'S EPISCOPAL CHURCH

St. John's Episcopal Church has the distinction of being the oldest Episcopal Church building in Montgomery County in continuous use. The church was established on June 22, 1842, on land donated by Ignatius and Eliza Waters.

The original church had four windows on each side. Until 1957 the building was located on the Georgia Avenue side of the church property with an entrance that faced Route 108. In 1910 the building, which had been put on rollers, was hauled to its present site by mules. Members added a sacristy, bell tower, vestibule and stained glass memorial windows. In 1980 the church was enlarged once again. Throughout these renovations the original altar window donated in 1867 was left untouched and is still located in the west transept.

The Parish Hall was completed in 1956. A day school with 22 pupils was opened in 1961. A new school building was erected and dedicated in 1964.

Each year during the Easter season, St. John's distributes millions of palm crosses to churches of all denominations throughout the country. The practice was begun by Reverend Alan Talbot, an Englishman who had served as a missionary in southeast Tanzania. Talbot thought that impoverished villagers could make palm crosses to subsidize their farming income. After selling the crosses to friends and churches in London for Palm Sunday, the project spread throughout Great Britain, the United States, Canada, Sweden and Australia.

The women of St. John's adopted the project in 1976. They distribute palm crosses through orders received from other churches. Money raised goes to the African villagers for farming equipment, medical supplies and other projects.

OAKDALE EMORY UNITED METHODIST CHURCH

Methodism did not reach Montgomery County until the 1780s when Robert Strawbridge came to Frederick County. The early Methodist congregations were formed in the northwestern part of the county where practice of Methodist religion was strongest.

Members of Oakdale Emory can flip back the pages of history to 1801 when their first church was built at the intersection of Emory Lane and Cashell Road. Fourteen members met in the small frame building that overlooked surrounding farms. By 1878 the congregation, then known as Emory Methodist Church, had grown to 22 members.

Although records are sketchy for the next 30 years, growth of the congregation continued. By 1914 members had outgrown the original building. The cornerstone for a new church at the corner of Georgia Avenue and Emory Church Road was laid by members, and in 1915 services began at the new site. The original church was sold, and the old frame building was covered with stone. Today it serves as a private residence.

In the late 1940s the congregation changed its name to Oakdale Emory Methodist Church since their building was located in the Oakdale community. An educational building was constructed in 1962. By 1982 the membership had grown to 654, and once again the church needed a larger building. Parishioners moved into a new church at the same site in February 1987 with a membership that had climbed to over 900. The new building included a 300-seat hall, five-office complex, parlor and sanctuary, and a renovated two-story educational building.

NOURISHMENT FOR GROWTH

From the days of the early Maryland colonists, both education and religion enriched the lives of those who lived in Olney and nearby communities. These institutions provided strength to community members and served as the seeds for a farming community to flourish.

The Quaker Community of Sandy Spring set the tone for developing an educational system in upper Montgomery County that led to the public school system. Other religious denominations established schools to educate their children.

But long before the various denominations offered education, these first churches offered more than a religious setting of worship. The churches bound the community together through the services and the events they sponsored. They enriched the lives of the congregation by giving comfort, direction and the opportunity for social activity. Members also worked on projects to assist the less fortunate in the community.

In a less complicated and slower-paced time, religion provided direction for the growth of this farming village. Education and religion have served as the framework for the cultivation of the mind and the soul.

Chapter 7

THE GOLDEN AGE OF MEDICINE

When asked to describe the practice of medicine from the 1940s through the 1970s, a retired physician captured the spirit of the time when he said, "To my mind, it was the golden age of medicine."

Scientific discoveries were being made and improvements were gradually occurring in all branches of medicine. People were given medical care even if they couldn't pay. "You were proud to keep up with things, and you were proud to be able to do something more for your sick patients, because this is what you were supposed to do. This was the idea of a service profession," he said.

One of the good things happening at the hospital in Olney was the gradual integration of more scientific approaches to medical problems he said. Doctors kept up their education on the latest research and medical techniques by sharing knowledge with each other. Top-notch specialists came to the hospital from Baltimore and Washington, "and they brought their knowledge," of the most up-to-date procedures to share with the staff. "There was never any question of compensation for that," he said.

Education was a lot different then. "Now a days they have all these very fancy courses that cost thousands of dollars to attend. Doctors come and are highly paid for giving the courses," he said. "Back in that time there was never any question about paying one another for extracting some of the knowledge that they may have. I knew some things that other doctors didn't know. There were many specialists who knew things that none of us general practitioners knew."

Medicine was different in those days too. "We had ideals and these were shared by all the doctors. There was never any question that you would patent a discovery that you might make, or a new medication or medical instrumentation. You felt very lucky if something got named after you but there was never any question of making money."

EARLY 20TH CENTURY MEDICAL CARE

Before 1920 medical care was not so readily available in Olney. When hospitalization was needed, residents were forced to make an exhausting trip to Baltimore or Washington.

The trip required patients to climb into a horse and wagon or jalopy for a journey to the railroad station. Patients boarded a train into the city. Upon arrival the sick traveler again sought transportation to the hospital. Imagine feeling sick or in pain with no option except to make such a demanding journey. It would seem that the trip could only further deteriorate health and certainly deplete the stamina so important for recovery.

THE ERA OF DR. BIRD

But that all changed when Jacob Wheeler Bird, M.D. (1885-1959) arrived in Olney in 1909. He came from Baltimore in a horse-drawn buggy with brand new rubber tires. The 23-year-old doctor had earned his medical degree from the University of Maryland at Baltimore. Bird had two years experience -- one as an intern and another as senior resident at the University Hospital in Baltimore. When Bird came to the Olney area, he saw open farmland and a small, rural community. He found a half-dozen or so elderly physicians practicing medicine in an area that stretched from Brookeville south to Olney, east to Spencerville and into Howard County.

Bird's uncle had told the young doctor about the recent death of a local physician, Dr. Roger Brooke. Bird's uncle had also advised him that the nearby Sandy Spring community would make a fine neighborhood for a home.

Mrs. Brooke, widow of the late Dr. Brooke, had interviewed several doctors to take over her husband's practice. But she liked the young doctor and hoped he would accept. "Dr. Bird, I hope thee will come," she wrote in a letter. "All the others ask me how much money they could make and thee asks me what kind of a place this is to live in."

Bird bought Mrs. Brooke's Olney home which still stands on the road that bears his name. Typical of the day, Bird saw patients in his home. A glass-enclosed porch served as the patient waiting-room.

Mrs. Brooke's instincts about the young doctor were well-founded. Bird forged a career that brought residents and the medical profession together in the founding of a community hospital.

MONTGOMERY GENERAL HOSPITAL

By 1916, just a few years after Bird began practicing medicine here, the young doctor realized just how much a hospital was needed. Bird rented a small private house, Wrenwood, and set up a five-bed hospital. The house was located on New Hampshire Avenue in the village of Brinklow between Ashton and Brighton. In just two years the small facility served almost 150 patients, and Bird felt certain a community hospital could be successful.

The timing for a hospital building campaign could not have been worse. It was 1918 and World War I was raging. Men had been drafted for the war effort, and women were left to perform the chores of the missing farm hands. Despite these problems, Bird assembled a group of residents and presented his idea for a hospital.

Bird worried about the response of residents to his idea. Determined to become a surgeon, Bird knew that he could not remain in the community without a nearby hospital. He presented his plan and often recounted the story of his anxiety as he awaited the group's response. He described how his heart sank with the long silence that followed his talk. But a farmer from Spencerville, Robert H. Miller, led the way by pledging $100 if others would too. Many in the group followed his lead. A corporation was formed, and non-profit stock was issued for $10 a share that raised $40,000. These stock certificates were purchased as a charitable contribution, an investment in the neighborhood. No one ever thought the stock was a financial investment. Bird began an era of strong community support that continues to this day.

The *Annals of Sandy Spring* chronicle the birth and growth of the hospital and reveal that Bird was not the first doctor to dream of a hospital in upper Montgomery County. Dr. William E. Magruder who died around the turn of the century had hoped to build a hospital on the site of his residence, Hermon, which was centrally located along Route 108.

"His hopes were never realized," wrote the recorder in the Annals, "but it seems particularly fitting that, as he was the originator of the idea, his plan should be carried out by those who came after him." Magruder's widow, Margaret, sold Hermon to the stock company that had been formed. Montgomery County General Hospital, as it was first called, was built among a stand of oak trees

PHOTO 11 The original Montgomery General Hospital that was built in 1920. The building was demolished in the early 1970s when a new hospital was built. Photo courtesy of Montgomery General Hospital.

on Route #108 across the street from present-day St. Peter's Catholic Church.

The recorder of the Annals struck the right cord. It was particularly fitting that Dr. Magruder's dream was fulfilled. Not only was Hermon the site of the first hospital in upper Montgomery County, but his house was incorporated into the medical facility. As the hospital grew, the section that formerly had been Dr. Magruder's house served many useful purposes -- as a nurses' residence, an office of the health department and a doctor's lounge.

However building the hospital did not go smoothly. The cornerstone was laid on May 31, 1919, but because of the war, there were delays in delivery of construction and medical supplies. By February 1920 a flu epidemic gripped the country for the second winter in a row. Entire families were sick and dying because of lack of nursing and proper food. The emergency forced the unfinished hospital to open its doors on February 6 of that year.

Community support for the hospital was evident from the start. A volunteer group, The Ladies' Auxiliary, later renamed the Women's Board, was organized in 1919. Volunteers worked for many days to prepare the facility for patients that would need care.

Anna Farquhar, one volunteer, wrote that "the furniture was in the building, crated and packed as it had been shipped...but there was no hospital equipment...no hot water bags, nor ice caps, no bed pans, no dishes...worst of all, no water in the building." A bathtub was dragged into the hospital and kept filled with fresh water.

"We went out into the highways and byways," Farquhar said, "(and) begged, borrowed and bought the necessities and by next afternoon there were five patients brought in through one of the worst blizzards of that winter." By years end the 28-bed facility admitted 596 patients. The charge for a semi-private room was $3.57.

Over the years, the women's volunteer group has been the hospital's mainstay -- dedicated to its support and promotion. Members did anything that needed doing. In past years volunteers performed tasks almost unheard of today -- rolling thousands of surgical dressings and canning cases of fruits and vegetables for patients.

For many years the Saturday after Thanksgiving was donation day. Home grown and canned vegetables and fruits, homemade jams and linens were donated for hospital patients. The *Handbook of the Women's Board of Montgomery General Hospital* (1987-88) listed the following donations for the year 1959: 352 qts. of home canned food; 130 pts. of jelly; 3,100 cases of food; 1 case of frozen orange juice and 8 qts. of frozen beans." Their earliest record of 1933 listed, "982 qts. of home canned fruit, 258 glasses of jelly and 852 tins were received. The largest amount of home canned (goods) was in 1942 with 1,761 qts."

Accounts of the hospital's history show other donations from community members. The Annals list bassinets, an iron lung and rooms that were endowed as memorials. Even the driveway in front of the old hospital on Route 108 that is still in place today was a donation -- a memorial to Frank M. Hallowell, killed in a Sandy Spring bank robbery in the early 1920s.

As the number of patients served by the hospital increased, Bird sought community support once again. In 1937 he asked residents for help to raise money to refurbish the hospital and to build a nurses' residence. Again the community supported the doctor, and a brick building was constructed on the corner of Route 108 and Prince Philip Drive. Today the building is a thrift shop that is run by the Women's Board.

During the campaign to raise money, Bird announced that 85 percent of the patients at the hospital came from a distance farther than five miles away. In just 17 years the hospital had earned the status of a regional facility.

In the early days of the hospital, the superintendent lived in the building. She ran the hospital and served as telephone operator and x-ray technician. She filled in on the floor when a nurse was absent and even assisted in the operating room when the nurse couldn't be there.

THE PRACTICE OF MEDICINE CHANGES

During the hospital's steady growth, there were changes in medical practice in the community. A doctor who came to the Olney area in the 1940s and initially practiced with Bird said the changes were dramatic from the 1940s, through the 1970s. "We didn't have penicillin when I first practiced here," he said. Although penicillin was developed years earlier, it was almost entirely limited to the armed services until after World War II, he explained. It first became available for public use in the late 1940s. "It was a piddling little bit and we gave piddling small doses compared to what came later," he said.

The antibiotic era brought major change to the practice of medicine. Physicians learned as much as possible about new treatment and techniques, and they practiced the best they could. As new discoveries were made, they tried to incorporate them into their practice. People expected less from a physician. They wanted to feel better and wanted relief, but they didn't necessarily expect to be cured. "Today they expect to be cured of everything, preferably in one office visit," a retired physician commented.

During those years doctors practiced medicine from an office in a wing of their home. Two dollars paid for the office visit in the late 1940s. It was easier to reach physicians at their home-offices because a family member was usually home even if the doctor was out. After doctors stopped using home-offices, the practice of medicine became more impersonal.

It was also the era of house calls. Five dollars paid for a home visit when patients were too ill to come to the office. But not every household had a telephone to call a doctor. If a physician was seeing a patient who did not have a telephone, he might return to his home office before learning another resident where he had just been also needed medical help. So doctors and residents developed an innovative way to communicate.One way to keep in touch was to display a signal in a prominent place. The Brookeville Post Office would hang a blue flag out in front of the building to let a passing doctor know he should stop and call his home-office.

The local central telephone operator was another way to get in touch with a doctor. The operator served as an "answering service." Physicians told the operator where they would be going so the operator could track them down for emergencies.

Until the mid 1950s the nearest large pharmacy was located in Rockville or Wheaton, which was a long drive. In the early 1900s J. Wallace Bond operated a small pharmacy from the corner of his Ashton store. He later moved his drugstore to his Ashton residence. Because of the small number of pharmacies, doctors carried and dispensed drugs as they visited patients. But all this changed when Alvin Berlin came to the village and opened a pharmacy on the northwest corner of the crossroads. Many of the doctors welcomed the new pharmacy because dispensing medicine was a money-losing proposition for them.

During those earlier years, Olney was a small community and the citizens pitched in to help in any way they could. A policeman, who is now retired, remembered sitting at the soda fountain at Berlin's Drug Store when someone rushed in to tell him about an auto accident. The officer went to the site of the crash and took the victim to the hospital. Apparently the hospital was short staffed and the officer had to assist the doctor in the operating room.

Originally Olney had no ambulances. If a patient needed transportation to the hospital, the doctor called a nearby funeral parlor to send a suitable vehicle.

Blood transfusions were not common, and the use of blood was rare in comparison to its use today. The kind of surgery performed was also different. According to retired doctors the hospital had some ability to transfuse blood in the late 1950s. But it was impractical for a small hospital to store large quantities of blood because of its short storage life.

So the citizens of the community helped when they were asked. People often knew their blood type, and the doctors knew the types of blood of various members of the community. When blood was needed, the person who had that blood type was called. Doctors took the blood from the donor, performed the necessary procedures and transfused the patient.

During the late 1940s and 1950s, a medical practice demanded long hours. Doctors performed surgery and made rounds in the morning. One physician recalled that he began office hours in early afternoon and frequently continued into the night, sometimes closing his office at 11 p.m.

Living in Olney and practicing medicine at a small country hospital might have been like a scene from the American classic, "Our Town," a play written by Thornton Wilder. It was a rural area removed from big city life. The air was clean and at night the darkness offered a lulling silence. The night was pitch black because there were no shopping centers nor street lights to illuminate the country roads.

Practicing medicine was a mutual experience between patient and doctor. Money was not a factor in either the medical or hospital practice. Doctors treated patients regardless of their ability to pay. The expenses of practicing medicine were few. In 1939 the hospital superintendent reported to the board of directors that 1441 patients had been admitted. More than 760 were free patients, a number that exceeded the paying patients.

But times changed. By the mid-1950s some doctors welcomed the trend toward an office away from home. With that change came some of the same expenses as in any small business such as high office rent. Malpractice insurance premiums began to rise, and today they are exorbitant. These costs have changed the practice of medicine, and doctoring has become more of a commodity than the service profession of the past.

In Olney the first medical offices outside of a doctor's home opened in 1955. The building housed a group of physicians and still stands on Route 108 just west of where the original hospital stood. The office building is easily recognized by the cupola on the roof. The 1950s also marked the end of Bird's long career. His outstanding contributions included the many surgical procedures he performed, assisted by Dr. Charles Tumbleson who served as anesthesiologist. Bird delivered some 4,000 babies, five on his own birthday of October 3rd. One of the many "Bird" babies as they were called eventually became a physician and began his practice with the doctor.

In 1959 the community honored Dr. Bird for 50 years of dedicated service. At the celebration the community presented him with a new Dodge Sedan, his 36th vehicle. His busy medical practice had taken a toll on previous cars. But the community soon mourned the doctor they loved. On October 25 of that year he and his wife were killed in an automobile accident in the Dodge Sedan while on a visit to Alabama.

Over the years the hospital continued to grow in size and services. New wings were added, and the final addition occurred in 1956. At the time the hospital had space for 80 beds. But the community continued to grow and finally outgrew the small hospital. Instead of more additions the board of directors voted to build a new facility. The original shareholders were located and their proxies were canceled. A corporation was formed. The name was shortened to Montgomery General Hospital from Montgomery County General Hospital, and community support was sought once again. A fund-raising campaign began and more than $2 million was raised. Together with a $5 million loan and a grant of almost $900,000, a new hospital on Prince Philip Drive was built.

In 1971 14 volunteer ambulances carried 39 patients from the old facility on Route 108 at the Hermon property to the current hospital. The new hospital had 158 beds but has grown to 229. Today it serves all ages with the latest techniques and most advanced technology. In 1990 the hospital admitted 9,168 patients and performed more than 500 procedures in the operating rooms each month. The 14-acre hospital campus includes a Cancer Treatment and Magnetic Resonance Imaging centers. The hospital is the largest Olney employer, offering more than 1,200 job opportunities.

THE WOMEN'S BOARD

When the Women's Board was initially founded, the eight charter members set the goals of providing volunteer service and also raising money for the hospital. Over the years, the board has sponsored several annual fund-raising events.

The board's longest running and most celebrated fund-raiser is the annual picnic and bazaar. Ever since July 1920 the last Tuesday in the month has been set aside for the all-day chicken dinner and bazaar.

The picnic began as a chicken supper, and the first event raised over $900. It was held at Sherwood High School and each year the number of suppers and revenues increased until more than 1,500 suppers were sold, raising thousands of dollars. In 1973 the board changed the supper to a picnic and bazaar to handle the increasing number of community members who supported the event. Today the fund raiser is held at Hermon, the grounds of the old hospital, and attracts thousands of visitors.

The event has never gone uncelebrated even during World War II. In 1943 amid gas rationing and food shortages, the Women's Board designed a clever plan for a "mystical" celebration of the annual supper. A certificate of attendance offering supper and an array of foods, games, dancing and bazaar items was sent to members of the community. Families selected from the items as if they were actually attending the supper and enclosed a check

Owing To War Conditions

THE ANNUAL SUPPER

of the

GENERAL HOSPITAL

MONTGOMERY COUNTY

under the direction of

THE WOMEN'S BOARD

formerly held at the

SANDY SPRING HIGH SCHOOL

WILL NOT TAKE PLACE IN 1944

WE HOPE, by circulating a "Letter", to receive financial assistance towards obtaining one or all of our major goals for 1944 — an operating room for emergency and minor operations — a remodeled diet kitchen — a new drug room — a freezing cabinet.

Figure 1 Announcement in the Women's Board handbook about the annual supper.

A Memory

— MENU —

FRIED CHICKEN or CHICKEN SALAD

HOME CURED HAM

MARYLAND BISCUITS ROLLS

SALADS

TOMATO SLAW POTATO

JELLY PICKLES

ICED TEA MILK COFFEE

Pony Rides - Fortune Telling - Bingo - Grag Bag - Fancy Work

Flowers - Ice Cream - Cakes - Lemonade - Food Specialties

THE WASHINGTON GAS-LIGHT BAND
DANCING AT 9 P. M.

A Reality

A hospital's ever present need is for newer and more modern equipment to ease the suffering of those who thru fate or fortune must enter its door. The Women's Board for many years has striven mightily towards obtaining these major and minor neccessities to both comfort and life. With the help of the Hospital's many kind friends they have accomplished much.

Do not forget the happy hours you spent at the supper — They will come again. Do not forget we still need your help — now as then.

Figure 2 Menu of the hospital supper that did not take place because of the war.

for the amount they would have spent. The citizens provided their yearly donation to the hospital, and in return, kept an unbroken record of attendance.

Today the Women's Board uses funds raised through events to support the hospital and an educational program. Preliminary figures from the 71st annual picnic/bazaar held in 1991 indicate the event grossed between $48,500 and $50,000. Volunteers fried 4,500 pounds of chicken, cooked 3,000 ears of corn, about 500 pounds of french fries and 300 pounds of beef barbecue.

One lifelong resident remarked, "My best childhood recollections here in the neighborhood were the hospital suppers we had on the last Tuesday in July." Recalling that time he remarked, "We kids would be volunteers, waiters and dishwashers, and the mother's would do the cooking, and everybody came and ate."

Since its founding more than 70 years ago, membership in the Women's Board has grown, and the services performed by the volunteers have changed. However some things remain the same. A sewing room at the hospital is still set aside where several women regularly meet to make bed curtains, covers for medical equipment and red stocking hats for babies born during the Christmas season.

The strong community support provided by the women volunteers has always been an invaluable resource to the hospital and is recorded for posterity. The Women's Board handbook for the year 1984 notes, "On May 8th the hospital administrator was presented with a plaque inscribed with the amount of monies we contributed to the new Montgomery General Hospital since its opening in 1971 -- $1,150,000; it hangs in the lobby."

Chapter 8

DEATH OF OLD OLNEY

Olney, from the early 1900s to the 1970s, carved a curious niche for itself. The village served the surrounding farming community and enticed visitors from Washington. Prominent government officials including presidents Franklin D. Roosevelt, Robert Taft and many statesmen delighted in dining at the Olney Inn. Yet local farmers still came to town to draw molasses from a wooden barrel at Hoyles Store, pick up mail at Soper's grocery, drop tools and machinery for repair at the blacksmith's, or get a price from the tinsmith to replace a barn roof. As the blacksmiths, tinsmiths and carpenters retired or died, new artisans took their places.

Over the years, ownership of the general stores changed. *The Annals of Sandy Spring* for 1900 lists several new owners for the establishments at the crossroads of Olney. Until the 1950s Olney didn't grow so much as adapt to the needs of the farming community. By and large Olney remained much the same.

It took a lot to change the old farming community, but finally it did change. Two major fires, suburban sprawl and the 1978 reconstruction of the Georgia Avenue/Route 108 intersection killed the rural village that reminded government officials and visitors of a step back in time -- of another way of life.

FINNEYFROCK BLACKSMITH SHOP

In 1885 Reuben P. Hines built a blacksmith shop on the southeast corner of the intersection. The original frame building with its brick forge was torn down for the road reconstruction. Dudley Finneyfrock, Hines' grandson, rebuilt the shop, but was not allowed to keep the old-style forge. Today he uses modern equipment for repairs. But Finneyfrock's shop does have reminders of the old Olney. In the office hand-forged farm tools hang from the walls of the brick building, and yellowed crumbling ledgers from the early days lean against modern account books.

PHOTO 12 A Christmas card sent by the Finneyfrock family, showing the old shop. Photo courtesy of Alvin (Doc) Berlin.

Hines had a simpler accounting system than his grandson. He kept handwritten accounts of what each customer owed him and collected once a year, probably at harvest. The old ledgers provide a sampling of costs throughout the years. Entries from 1890 show that shoeing a horse cost 60 cents. Twenty-four years later the price had risen to 80 cents, and by 1921 the cost was $1.20. Although Finneyfrock no longer shoes horses, he said that in the late 1980s the cost ranged from $45 to $85.

HINES HATCHERY

Some of the early settlers were innovative businessmen. They often had more than one business. Hines not only operated the blacksmith shop but farmed nearby property at what is now Hines Road and Georgia Avenue.

His wife was resourceful too. Around the turn of the century, Mrs. Hines began selling fresh-killed chickens and eggs from the basement of their house at the Oak Grove Poultry Farm, named after the towering oaks that shaded the property. In 1923, she moved to a shop on the west side of Georgia Avenue north of Old Baltimore Road.

Like many farmers in the communities of Olney and Sandy Spring, the Hines family kept up with technology. Their farm was one of the first to receive electricity under the National Rural Electric Project of the late 1920s. According to an old guest register kept by the family, representatives from the Philadelphia Electric Company and the Maryland University Extension Service came to learn how electricity provided advantages to farming.

Until the early 1980s school children visited the hatchery to see the process firsthand. They watched as eggs were placed in an incubator, chicks were hatched and the eggs were sorted and packaged for market. Today adults who had attended schools around Washington, D.C., fondly recall their school trips to see "the baby chicks" at Hines Hatchery.

In 1983, the hatchery stopped operating. The property was sold in a bankruptcy sale. Today a retail nursery occupies the site of the old hatchery.

MURPHY'S TINSMITH SHOP

It is sad to many long-time residents of Olney to see so little that is left of its past -- all in the name of progress. Like the hatchery, the tinsmith shop built in 1892 did not survive. However the shop was a going concern until the building was torn down for the 1978 widening of the Georgia Avenue/Route 108 intersection.

The tinsmith, Michael J. Murphy, had built his house and shop on the southwest corner of the intersection. The two-story, T-frame house faced north on Route 108. The attached tinsmith's shop and carriage barn faced east on Georgia Avenue, a toll road until the early 1900s. A toll booth sat aside the shop. When Albert Murphy (1891-1981) decided to follow his father's trade, he became an apprentice to a tinsmith in Libertytown and later joined his father in the Olney business.

Then, as well as today, sheet metal had a variety of uses. It could be shaped into many building materials, like gutters or pipe, and used for roofing. Metal roofs were popular in the 19th century on both houses and barns. The trick of installing a tin roof lay in carefully joining the pieces of sheet metal with standing seams so the roof would not leak.

Murphy, who drove an old green pick-up truck, was a familiar sight to area farmers and residents. Watching him perched on a steep roof repairing or replacing sections of tin even after he was well into his 80s, was not an uncommon sight to residents of the mid-1900s. Although Murphy didn't make decorative tinware, he occasionally made sheet metal liners for planters, covers for fireplaces, and probably soldered the metal milk cans for the dairy farmers.

HOYLES GENERAL STORE/BERLIN'S DRUG STORE

Across from Murphy on the northwest corner of the Route 108/Georgia Avenue intersection, William J. Hoyle operated a general store. Hoyle and his wife, Mattie, bought their old farmhouse around 1912 from the heirs of Jonathan Barnsley, an earlier resident. According to historic records, Barnsley built the structure as his residence when he married a second time in 1864.

The Hoyles renovated the first floor and used it for a dry goods store. The general store carried non-perishable staples such as flour and sugar, canned goods, and kerosene, as well as bolts of cloth, shoes, hardware and farming items. One resident recalled drawing molasses from a barrel at Hoyles.

Mattie Hoyle ran a boarding house on the second floor. Accommodations were available year-round. A post card advertisement from those days read "First-class Tourist Accommodations. Bath. Moderate rates...Phone Ashton 118-F-2-1."

In the mid-1950s the building where the Hoyles lived and operated their store was purchased by pharmacist Alvin Berlin, endearingly called "Doc Berlin." When Berlin's dad heard that his son was opening a drug store in the building, he was surprised. He didn't believe the sparsely-settled farming community would be a good investment for a store. "Sonny," said Berlin's dad, "where are the people going to come from?"

After renovations the old building took on a new life as the Olney Drug Store, a local spot that became an institution to many residents. Around 1954 when the pharmacy first opened, Berlin recalled that "now and then" a farmer would ride to his drug store on horseback.

Until Doc Berlin arrived, local physicians carried and dispensed medications as they made house visits, stocked medicines they needed in their offices, or had patients travel to the nearest pharmacy in Wheaton or Rockville. The Olney Drug Store provided a much-needed convenience to area doctors, veterinarians and residents. Besides ordering various prescrip-

PHOTO 13 Hoyle's Tourist Home, located at the northwest corner of the Olney intersection. Mrs. W.J. Hoyle offered moderate prices, meals and boarding. Photo courtesy of Alvin (Doc) Berlin.

tion and non-prescription drugs from pharmaceutical companies, Doc Berlin made medications from formulas he had devised

While the drug store was a place to get prescriptions filled, it also had a soda fountain. The store became the local meeting spot, and folks stopped by to chat, discuss problems of the day over a good cup of coffee, and get a milkshake or a quick meal. It was pitch black at night along the country road, and the lights of the drug store lit up the crossroads village.

At the Olney Drug Store local celebrities casually mixed with neighbors. Two baseball Hall of Famers from the Ashton and Sandy Spring areas, Jack Bentley and Sam Rice, visited the drug store. Both had played for the former Washington Senators. Berlin recalled that once Mr. America came in and needed two stools to sit at the counter because of his massive size.

The fountain was a popular spot for breakfast after Sunday morning church. The late Dean Acheson, who lived on a farm in Sandy Spring and served as Secretary of State under President Harry Truman, often stopped by to pick up the Sunday newspaper. Berlin also ordered "Francis Tex," a special non-oily hair tonic, Acheson used.

Doc Berlin likes to tell the story of how his drug store catered to President Johnson. One of Johnson's political advisors, Horace Busby, lived on Ednor Road across from Woodlawn. When the late president visited him, soft drinks, sandwiches and chips were ordered from the store. Doc Berlin also recalled the excitement that some of the president's visits would cause. Busby's neighbors told Berlin that when Johnson visited, the secret service would climb up and sit in the nearby trees, and the road would be blocked as they watched over the president.

Doc Berlin and his customers enjoyed trading stories about Olney, a town that was close to the bustle of a major city, but still portrayed an idyllic setting. Photographs of the roads at the intersection where the drug store sat from the mid 1950s through the end of the 1970s capture a farming community that depict a "canopy of trees" gently spreading across and above the two-lane country roads. But the drug store, too, was not to survive. Along with other buildings of the old Olney, it was torn down during the 1978 intersection widening. Many of the residents came to see the building bulldozed, and some got there early to take mementos of this institution. The remaining contents of the drug store including a wooden telephone booth and old medicine bottles were auctioned.

Doc Berlin opened a store in the Olney Shopping Center but the atmosphere never matched the "feel" of the old Olney Drug Store. A few years later Doc sold the business to other pharmacists. Eventually the drug store closed and, today, food and drug conglomerates compete with each other to fill the prescriptions of Olney's residents.

An old-timer said Olney is different now. Unlike the time when everyone knew everyone he explained, "I can come down to the Olney intersection and not recognize a face."

Progress has changed Olney -- the crossroads has become a major intersection. And Olney no longer has a popular meeting spot to stop and trade stories over a good cup of coffee.

SOPER'S STORE

Soper's Store, located on the northeast corner of the intersection, was a longtime fixture in the community. The original general store was built in the mid-1800s and was a going concern long before Robert P. Soper purchased it in 1912. As a teenager in 1891 he had actually worked for the previous owner, J.C. Williams. Soper moved to Baltimore, then returned in 1906 and rented the Williams General Store before purchasing it.

Soper sold a variety of grocery items to farmers and bought fresh vegetables, meat and ice from them to sell. By 1919 he was offering ice cream -- a popular treat -- year-round. Since the store was located in the center of town, Soper served as the postmaster, and the post office was in the store.

PHOTO 14 Soper's Store, located at the northeast corner of the Olney intersection. The building was built in the mid-1800s. Photo courtesy of Sandy Spring Museum.

Farmers not only came by for groceries each week, but stopped to pick up their mail. When automobiles became common, Soper added a gas pump for his customers' convenience. In 1945 he retired, and other businesses occupied the location. The building burned in July 1973, and the owner decided not to rebuild since the road widening would have destroyed a new building.

BURNS' GARAGE AND ARMSTRONG'S FEED STORE

At the turn of this century, many local residents were still dependent upon horse-drawn transportation. Those who wanted to go to Washington hopped a ride on a dairy truck that ran from Sandy Spring to downtown. But the dairy truck stopped running.

Around 1912 R.R. Moore of Sandy Spring started an auto truck route that picked up milk cans, farm products and people. Described in the Annals "the conveyance could scarcely be called stylish in appearance, and its seats might have been more comfortable, yet the public seemed glad to use even a milk can for a resting place..." However, the Sandy Spring auto truck line ceased operating in August 1914.

That same year Leonard Burns bought a house adjacent to Soper's Store and built a bus and truck garage. Burns, who was in his 20s at the time, started his bus and trucking line at an opportune time. Many riders of the old truck line were relieved that they would continue to have transportation. Older residents recalled that folks took the bus to work into Washington, D.C., especially during World War I. When the state finished paving the road between Ashton and Ellicott City, now Route 108, Burns began a jitney, a small bus service between Olney and Ellicott City where residents could catch a trolley or train service to Baltimore. Burns also provided bus trips for residents. In addition he had a trucking service that hauled cattle, grain or produce to market for the farmers. One truck was used strictly for taking milk cans to the dairies in Washington.

In the mid-1920s Burns sold the garage and house to Elmer G. Armstrong. He sold the busline to a Washington company. Then Burns bought a farm on Georgia Avenue, just south of the large house that would later become Olney Inn, and kept the dairy truck in service for several years.

Armstrong opened a feedstore in the building. He held a Southern States franchise and when Soper's Store closed in 1945, Armstrong became the postmaster. Several retired postal clerks recalled that the post office was located in one corner of the feed store. Customers, they said, often commented on the smell of feed when they came to get their mail.

Working in the building wasn't easy. The postal personnel had to scrub the floor of the post office section every Saturday. And there were no bathroom facilities in the building. When Armstrong retired in the 1960s, the post office leased and remodeled the building. Armstrong sold the property in 1973 to

William Scaggs, owner of the Anchor Inn Restaurant in Wheaton. The post office had to look for other quarters. The U.S. Postal Service bought land west of the intersection on the southside of Route 108, and the new Olney Post Office opened in 1975.

D.G.S. GROCERY

The D.G.S. grocery store, located in the old Farmers' Grange Hall on the southeast corner of the Olney intersection, had a romantic beginning and a sad ending. The story began when Francis Hawkins met an attractive young woman who was the tutor for the daughter of Clara Mae Downey, owner of the Olney Inn. When the two decided to marry, Downey gave them a large wedding and reception at the inn. She also offered to help them establish a grocery store in the grange hall that she owned. Hawkins took a two-year lease on another grocery store in the southwest quadrant of the intersection while he and his father renovated the old grange hall.

They put a brick veneer on the wooden building, which had been built like a barn, and made the second floor into an apartment. Hawkins and his wife moved into the apartment and opened the new D.G.S. Grocery in 1936.

During the next few years Hawkins made additions to the building. The first was a three-story concrete section at the rear, which served as a warehouse with expanded second floor family quarters. Several years later he built another addition for a frozen food locker. Hawkins was one of the first grocers in the area to offer a frozen food plan to customers and worked with Sears Roebuck to promote freezer use. He also offered freezer lockers for rent so area farmers could freeze large quantities of meat and vegetables for later use.

The widening of the Olney intersection forced Hawkins out of business. Since his building stood in the way of the future road, it too was torn down.

OLNEY INN

But it was the Olney Inn that captured the imagination and interest of local residents and government officials. The rambling frame structure stood amid towering oak, maple and walnut trees. From its accidental beginning to the suspicious fire that gutted it, the inn left an indelible mark on Olney.

The inn was initially a farmhouse called Mount Olney that was built in 1875 by Granville Farquhar. It was named Mount Olney because the property was said to be the same height as the Washington Monument, 555 feet high. Situated on a knoll, the farmhouse offered a lovely view in all directions.

Following Farquhar's death in 1915, the farm was sold to the blacksmith, Reuben Hines. He farmed the land for about 10 years until Clara May Downey of Houston, Texas, got a flat tire while she was driving through the Olney countryside.

Downey had recently moved to Washington and wanted to start her own business as well as live in the country. A tearoom, she decided, would be the answer. However Downey had an impressive resume that would fit most any business. During World War I she had helped in the organization of the U.S. Air Service and had studied management and organization at Columbia University.

During her search for a location, Downey drove on all major roads within a 20-mile radius of Washington. While waiting to have her flat tire fixed in Olney, she looked around and liked what she saw. She bought the Mount Olney farmhouse and 40 acres of land from Hines in 1925 for $14,000.

The inn opened in May 1926 with a staff of three and three tables that seated four each. The original summer kitchen fireplace was used for cooking and Downey grew all the produce on the farm. The farm also had coops for chickens and pig pens. Hams, too, were cured and prepared at the farm.

Downey, who lived on the second floor of the inn, quickly built a fine reputation. On opening day the inn served two guests. The next day 35 were served and just six months later 3,500 people had come through the doors at the inn.

In 1930 Downey remodeled the inn and made the original summer kitchen into the entrance hall. She added a dining room and invited Oskar Hauenstein, a Viennese artist, to paint scenes of Maryland on the walls. In the inn's heyday 13 murals depicting Maryland's history from the colonists' first landing at St. Mary's to the first steam locomotive on the Baltimore and Ohio Railroad graced the walls. One mural included a scene of the Sandy Spring Meeting House. When the renovation and decoration was completed, 350 people could be seated.

The inn had a lovely setting. Nestled among trees, the property had a vast expanse of orchards and a beautiful flower garden. From the 1930s through the 1960s numerous public officials and foreign visitors dined at the inn. According to accounts from retired inn personnel, President Roosevelt ate there twice a

PHOTO 15 The Olney Inn in 1975, several years before it burned. Photo courtesy of the Park Historian's Office, Maryland-National Capital Park and Planning Commission.

PHOTO 16 Another view of the Olney Inn, showing the grounds and the addition that was added. Photo courtesy of the Sandy Spring Museum.

----

month and a ramp was built for his wheelchair. His favorite meal was said to be the "Southern Smothered Chicken."

Downey's daughter, Grace wrote a newspaper article about the inn many years after her mother was no longer the proprietor. In the article she recalled one particular visit by the president. "A highlight of the inn's history was the visit made by President Roosevelt," she wrote. "No one except Mrs. Downey and her mother knew he was to be entertained at a party arranged by Secretary of the Treasury Morgenthau. When the waiters entered with their laden trays, one of them spied the President and exclaimed 'Good Laws, the President of the United States!' It's claimed (the waiter) fainted and fried chicken went everywhere."

Several First Ladies frequented the inn. Newspaper accounts record visits by Eleanor Roosevelt, Lady Bird Johnson, Mamie Eisenhower and Bess Truman. Richard Nixon, when he was vice president, also ate at the inn. So many well-known Washington figures and foreign dignitaries came to the inn that a former hostess started collecting their signatures. She recalled that the former Shaw of Iran visited, and the owner at the time, Allison Brewster, took out the best china and crystal for him.

In the early years Downey only operated the Olney Inn during the summer months. In 1935 she opened another restaurant which she ran during the winter in Miami Beach, Florida, and also called it Olney Inn. In 1941 she chose New York City as the location for a third Olney Inn.

World War II brought two of the inns to a halt. The New York City restaurant closed, never again to reopen. The inn here in Olney shut down temporarily because of gas rationing. But Downey continued to run the Miami Beach establishment

In 1946 Downey renovated the inn at Olney once again, and reopened. Two years later she developed a resort in Islamorada, Florida, and named it Olney Inn. Downey sold the Olney restaurant in 1950 to Katharine Weiniger who ran it for four years. The following owner, Allison Brewster, continued the fame of the inn for the next 12 years. While Brewster owned the property, she renovated the old barn which operated as an antique shop for a time.

When DeWitt Yates and Roy and Ray Graham took over the inn, they sold some of the acreage that had been used as orchards, chicken coops and pig pens. The inn's last owner, Harry Simms, was in the process of selling the property when a leaf pile beside the building ignited and engulfed the 134-year old structure. Because the building was so old there were no fire walls to contain the flames. Newspaper accounts of the incident reported that over 100 firetrucks were at the scene in an attempt to save the building.

Two days after the fire, many Olney residents and former inn guests paid their final respects to the historic building. They gathered at the gutted structure and in a moving final visit, walked in a candle and flashlight vigil around the property. Articles about the event tell how residents expressed their sorrow and anger over the fire. Newspaper headlines about the blaze also invoked emotional feelings. One simply said, "Olney has lost a friend," and another said, "Olney Inn eulogized by many." Curiously enough, two electrified gas lampposts from the inn have survived. Several years before the fire, one of the inn owners brought four broken lampposts to Dudley Finneyfrock's blacksmith shop for repair. Finneyfrock made two lampposts from the pieces he had, but no one ever picked them up. Finneyfrock donated them to the Sandy Spring Museum, and today the towering lamps glow at the entrance to the museum's herb garden.

Just one year before the Olney Inn fire, the 1700s Fair Hill farmhouse also burned down under suspicious circumstances. With the burning of the two historic structures and the razing of the blacksmith and tinsmith shops, the drug store and D.G.S. grocery, the core of old Olney was gone. Shopping centers and the headquarters of a bank sprang up to serve the new families moving to the "country." But by then, very little of Olney's rural life was left. The village that served the farming community had died.

Chapter 9

THE COMMUNITY'S FOUNDATION

Although Olney is not an incorporated town, many institutions bind the community together -- a theater, library, museum, fire department and recreation center. Some organizations like the museum and fire department originated in Sandy Spring and expanded to Olney. Others such as the theater and recreation center sprouted in the Olney community.

OLNEY THEATRE

Today Olney Theatre, the official State Summer Theater of Maryland, has earned a rich reputation for excellent performances in the Washington-Baltimore area. Opening nights are regularly reviewed in *The Washington Post,* and the theater is often recognized at the annual Helen Hayes awards ceremony. But the theater was not always welcome. Initially suspicion greeted the outsiders who wanted to establish a theater on an Olney farm.

The Annals of Sandy Spring for 1936 painted a wary verbal picture of what might happen if the old Davis property on Route 108 became a theater. The recorder for that year wrote, "It is said he [new owner Steven Cochran of Washington, D.C.] is to build a summer theater and dramatic school, while the neighborhood looks on with apprehension and bated breath. Let us hope it is not the entering wedge to end our serene and rural character."

This initial fear must have prompted recorders of the Annals to keep a sharp eye on happenings at the new theater. The next entry noted, "On March 21 [1938] an article appeared in The Washington Post, stating that the Olney Theater Corporation was ready to start their new project...Miss Ethel Barrymore, who is to be one of the directors, was here looking over the situation."

On July 25, 1938, the Annals announced that the theater opened with Ellisa Landi in the play, "The Lady Has a Heart." Theater records indicate that both barn dances and summer stock took place at the theater in the early days, and the building was described as resembling a pavilion more than an actual theater.

For the next several years the Annals remained silent about the playhouse. But in fall of 1941 the Annals noted, "The neighborhood woke up when they found that Mr. Stephen Cochran had been joined in partnership by Mr. C.Y. Stephens of Washington, and that their plans included an addition to the theater and the old Davis home. The house was to be surrounded with commodious porches to be used as a restaurant."

C.Y. Stephens, the new co-owner, was a businessman and philanthropist who owned the High's Dairy chain in Washington. Although he had studied agriculture at Iowa Sate University, Stephens had a keen interest in and appreciation of good drama. However, his enthusiasm for the new theater project was not universally shared.

Residents who were unhappy with plans to expand the theater made it known. After discovering a legal loophole, they forced

PHOTO 17 The Olney Theatre as it looked from the mid-1940s until 1990. The theatre has been renovated and a lobby has been added. Photo courtesy of the Sandy Spring Museum.

Stephens to stop work. Later they voiced their opposition at a zoning board hearing, but their effort failed to stop the expansion project.

When the theater reopened in 1942, the old farmhouse on the property became a restaurant. But World War II ruined the new theater's first-night opening that May. The federal government declared gas rationing on May 17 for 17 states on the Eastern Seaboard. The next day the theater opened with "George Washington Slept Here," but according to the Annals few seats were filled in the audience. Since the theater drew patrons from Washington and Baltimore, Stephens decided to close the facility for the duration. Oddly enough Harold Ickes of Olney, who served as petroleum administrator during the war, had recommended gas rationing.

Following the war in 1946 Stephens reopened the theater with the "package" productions that were popular during that era. These plays, performed in a succession of theaters throughout the summer, featured a well-known star. The renovated farmhouse that had a short life as a restaurant became an actors' residence.

The magic of Helen Hayes in "Good Housekeeping," launched Olney Theatre's next opening night. The theater hosted a parade of stars for the next seven years as Lillian Gish, John Carradine and Basil Rathbone stepped onto the Olney stage.

In 1949 Sarah Churchill made her American debut in a benefit performance of "The Philadelphia Story." Seated in the audience were President Harry Truman and his wife, Bess.

The actors' residence has been a temporary home to many well-known performers. Burl Ives, Jessica Tandy, Hume Cronyn, Moss Hart and Jose Ferrer are but a few performers who spent time there, and some have left bits of their personal history. According to stories, fellow actors at the residence had to find separate lodging for Tallulah Bankhead because she kept everyone awake late at night with her boisterous and unruly antics. A deserted stone gas station on the property along Route 108 was made into a guest cottage specifically for her. Another account said that Bankhead stopped the traffic on Route 108 when she disrobed and wandered onto the highway. Today the small residence is called the "star cottage" and serves as an alternative to the actors' residence.

Olney Theatre historians also mention other actors and actresses who appeared at the Olney Theatre. Jose Ferrer enjoyed cooking his specialty, paella, and serving the dish to the actors at the residence. TV star Pernell Roberts got his start at the theater with a walk-on role and appeared in several other productions. Carol Channing, Nancy Davis Reagan, John McGiver and Olympia Dukakis are other well-known performers who appeared at the theater early in their careers.

By 1953 Stephens had grown tired of the "hot-weather comedies," that featured stars but not the best performances. He asked his accountant, Benny Goodman, for advice. Goodman told Stephens about Father Gilbert V. Hartke (1907-1986), founder of the drama department at Catholic University. Goodman thought Hartke had the experience to both manage the theatre and produce original plays. According to theater records Stephens enjoyed telling the story that a Jewish accountant counseled the son of a Baptist minister to give his theater to a Catholic priest.

Hartke led the theater in a new direction. Under his guidance more serious works were performed and premieres of new plays were featured. Gradually the theater expanded its season and increased the number of performances for each show.

One show premier attracted football fans to the theater. In 1992 John Riggins, former running back for the Washington Redskins and a member of the Football Hall of Fame, played a major role in "Illegal Motion." In a television interview Riggins talked about the role as a coach in the Olney Theatre production and commented, "There aren't many [football players] who have won an Oscar, but I'm going to be the first."

The setting of the theater is a rustic building with peach baskets that frame the lights. Up until the 1960s, an oak tree grew inside the building and its top stretched up through the roof. When it rained, water dribbled down the tree trunk. The tree was finally removed. In the mid-1980s another incident highlighted the theater's rustic setting. During a performance of "Deathtrap," a big black snake dropped onto the center of the stage.

Of course the actors' residence has a ghost, who prefers Room 3. According to producing director Bill Graham, Jr., weird sounds have been heard coming from the room and stories of unidentifiable figures walking through the closed door of Room 3 have been reported.

Today the theater is an independent, non-profit organization that depends upon monies from admissions, grants and gifts to produce plays. An expansion and renovation program begun in the early 1990s offers the prospect of year-round performances in the future.

F.O.O.T.

Friends of the Olney Theatre (F.O.O.T) was formed by a group of supporters in 1986. They have raised thousands of dollars for the playhouse through several fund-raising events. Their efforts have allowed the theater to upgrade the heating and air conditioning system and renovate the Actors' Residence.

NATIONAL PLAYERS

National Players is the touring arm of the Olney Theatre. The late Rev. Gilbert V. Hartke founded the group in 1949. Hartke selected the most talented drama students, gave them special training, and sent them to towns and schools that didn't have access to classical theater. National Players has grown, and today it is part of the Olney Theatre Corporation. Members perform two plays a year in over 30 states east of the Rocky Mountains.

For young actors and actresses who have completed college drama classes, this one-year season is a chance to discover if they are really cut out for the professional stage. The 12- to 16-member company is chosen through a national talent search. The group practices two shows, one Shakespearian and one contemporary, for about seven weeks. These young performers take their show on the road and play to audiences of all sizes and levels of sophistication -- from 200 enthusiasts in a high-school cafeteria in Brooklyn, N.Y., to 1,700 devotees at National Theatre in Washington, D.C.

The performers travel in a 30,000-pound diesel truck, loaded with sets and costumes. After they set up the stage, one of the performers acts as stage manager. The sponsors in each community decide which of the two shows will be performed, although often, the troupe is asked to perform both plays. National Players is probably the longest running classical touring company in the country.

LONGWOOD RECREATION CENTER

The popular recreation center, on the west side of Georgia Avenue a few miles north of the Olney intersection, hosts many activities of the county's recreation department. The center's origin is an outstanding example of civic activism at its best.

George F. Kimmell, a prominent Washington patent attorney, bought the historic Longwood house and property in 1935. He founded the private Longwood School for Boys in 1946 and constructed several buildings on the property including an administration building, hall, gym and dormitories. The gym that has four columns and a pediment is part of Longwood Recreation Center today and is the only school building that has survived. The school brochure for the 1947-48 year says it was founded "upon the premise that coincident with a sound formal education and character training, there must be an adequate health and physical development program...to equip a boy with the confident self-discipline that is needed in a world of post-war tension and uncertainty." Kimmell hoped the school would prepare students who wanted to go to prestigious schools like the Naval Academy at Annapolis and the Military Academy at West Point.

The school brochure listed sports and recreational facilities that included a lake for fishing, a diving board, rafts and canoes. A nine-hole golf course was under construction, the brochure said, and athletic fields and a gym were available.

The school could serve 80 students, 50 boarders and 30 commuters. Tuition for boarding students was $1,250. Charges for day students was $600 plus fees. Longwood School for Boys opened in 1947 but closed after three years.

In 1951 Kimmell leased the school facilities to the federal government. The Civil Defense Administration taught defense techniques at the site. The agency built what looked like streets of bombed-out buildings to practice rescue operations recalled a local historian. By 1963 the government vacated the site, and it sat desolate and unattended.

About 10 years later Barbara Truex, then an Olney resident, looked at the abandoned building and wondered if it could be converted into a community center. The Longwood Advisory Committee was established to organize the community and persuade the county council to buy the property. When Truex moved, Ben Santaiti of Olney assumed chairmanship of the committee.

Unfortunately severe inflation and a tight budget gripped Montgomery County in the mid-1970s. In addition county officials did not agree with the advisory committee on the type of facility the community wanted, and costs for the project escalated. The project was cut from the county's budget several times.

The advisory committee wanted the gym renovated and a section added for a kitchen, weight-exercise rooms, multi-purpose room and space for arts, crafts and educational programs. But county officials questioned the need for the addition and for exterior facilities such as the ballfields that the committee wanted.

Finally, the advisory committee convinced the county council that the project could be completed in two stages -- gym renovation and addition. The committee offered to raise $16,000 for stage one. For the next 18 months individuals and civic organizations held skateboard and golf tournaments, door-to-door campaigns, parties, dances, raffles, craft fairs and crab feasts. By the time the first phase of gym restoration was completed and dedicated in June 1978, the community had raised almost $33,000 for the project.

The second stage addition was completed in 1982. Today the building is in continual use. Meetings, receptions and banquets are held by numerous groups. The county recreation department also offers a wide range of programs for all ages, from preschool to senior citizens.

THE OLNEY COMMUNITY LIBRARY

Although located in Olney, the library has its roots in Sandy Spring. The Quaker community always placed a high value upon education and exhibited a passion for reading.

The Annals frequently mention lending libraries or book clubs that were established in the community. But perhaps the most frustrating chronicle is the on-again, off-again history of the community library.

In 1842 prospects looked bright for the newly established, Sandy Spring Library Company, set up in a room adjoining the Sandy Spring Store. By 1883 the Sherwood Friends School gave the library one of its rooms until a library building was built in 1887. That building on Route 108 stood between the old Montgomery Mutual Insurance Company building and the Sandy Spring National Bank. Residents paid a fee to belong to the library company. However by 1895 the library was in financial trouble and closed. An entry in The Annals for 1895 noted that a successful entertainment was held to benefit the defunct library and the debts were paid.

For a community that so loved to read, the library's financial troubles, no doubt, must have been frustrating. Interest in circulating the books once again surged in the summer of 1899 when two residents reopened the library one day a week. But the library closed, and eventually the books were transferred to the Community House on Meeting House Road. In 1914 the library building was moved to a site behind the Sandy Spring store and was torn down in 1935.

The Sandy Spring community tried again in 1948. The Sherwood Library Association was established. Donations and membership fees provided the library with operating funds, and the old Sherwood School provided space for the library. Three years later the Sherwood Library and six other independent libraries gave their assets to the county to establish the Montgomery County Library system.

The county bought the abandoned Ashton Meeting House, built in 1893, and the books were moved from the adjacent Sherwood School. The old meeting house was a small white frame building with limited space. A former librarian recalled that the bathroom served as a staff room because most of the space had to be used for books. Only 10 cars fit in the small parking lot.

As the population of nearby Olney grew, the library system added a bookmobile stop at the intersection of Georgia Avenue and Route 108. However the Olney community wanted its own library. The county purchased the present library site on Route 108 just west of the Georgia Avenue/Route 108 intersection in 1979, but residents were unhappy with the county's delay in starting construction of the building. The community launched a massive petition drive. Over 4,300 signatures were collected, which persuaded county officials to begin construction three years sooner than planned.

A picture of the ground-breaking ceremony in March 1981 shows county officials standing in a field of hay stubble, shivering in heavy winter coats. Thirteen months later the Sherwood facility closed, and library staff and area residents boxed and transported the 12,000 books to the new building. The library system provided additional books, and on opening day in May 1982, patrons could select from about 30,000 publications.

The new building has 15,000 square feet of space compared to the 2,100 square feet at the old Sherwood facility. The library staff must have been delighted with the separate staff room and large work area where they could prepare books for circulation. Residents finally had a real library with many more books, magazines and newspapers.

Several years later the old Sherwood Library building was moved to the Sandy Spring Friends School campus. Today the school uses the building for a variety of activities.

THE SANDY SPRING
VOLUNTEER FIRE DEPARTMENT

The threat of fire produced an alarming fear in rural communities in the 1800s and early 1900s. If a barn or house caught fire, there was no quick way of getting help. By the time assistance from the neighboring farms arrived, the roaring flames often kept "firefighters" at a distance. Pouring buckets of water on the outer edges of the burning structure to contain the fire was all the firefighters could do. The bucket brigade -- a line of neighbors passing along buckets of water -- was the usual way of squelching fires.

Area residents unanimously agreed that something had to be done to protect themselves from fire, but they could not agree on a best solution. "There has been much talk of a fire engine for the neighborhood," read the Annals in 1923, "but with such great distances, the likelihood of its being in the wrong place at the right time seemed too great..."

The young men's club at St. John's Episcopal Church and the American Legion Post in Brookeville also debated the issue.

Eventually the church group initiated the placement of hand-operated pump tanks throughout the area.

In November 1923 community leaders in Sandy Spring met with representatives from the established fire departments in Rockville and Silver Spring. The two departments encouraged the Sandy Springers to organize a fire company and to purchase a small truck. At subsequent meetings the organizing committee wrestled with the problems of raising money to buy a fire engine, incorporating, and finding a home for their future department. The men refused to order an engine until they had raised a certain portion of its cost. A. Douglas Farquhar, who became the first fire chief, noted that information about a siren system was thrown into the trashcan because the committee had not yet gotten to that stage.

But the organizing committee was driven to accomplish the task at hand. Even before the first public organizational meeting was held, the committee had initiated a fund-raising campaign, ordered a maroon fire engine and persuaded Montgomery Mutual Insurance Company in Sandy Spring to convert part of the old horse shed into a garage for the engine. By early September 1924 the committee was ready to go public. About 50 people attended a meeting at Sherwood High School and voted to formally organize. The Sandy Spring Volunteer Fire Department became the fourth volunteer fire unit in Montgomery County.

The early firefighters were farmers and local businessmen who had no formal training. They learned fire-fighting skills on the job and from each other.

The early fire engines were converted Model T Fords or pick up trucks. Chemical tanks were added to the engines. The tanks held a mixture of baking soda and acidic acid that created pressure to force the water out of the tank. However when the firefighters added the chemical mixture to the water, the chemicals ate through their clothing. A breathing apparatus had not yet been invented for firefighters and the volunteers quickly became known as "leather lungs."

A November 14, 1974, article in the County Courier honoring Spencer Brown for his 77th birthday celebration noted that Brown helped found five fire departments including Sandy Spring's. In the article Brown explained that the first fire truck was an International Chemical Truck and described the vehicle. "I believe we got that truck in the fall of '24. You had to mix the soda and acid in two 30-gallon water tanks. That stuff really ate up your clothes," Brown said.

"When you grabbed the wheel of the tank after mixing the soda and acid, you'd better be ready to shoot it, cause it had to go somewhere, it was under pressure you know." Brown said the tanks were like the soda-acid fire extinguishers of earlier days. He added, "We've had our ups and downs in the Sandy Spring department, a lot of hard work before we even had radios...a local operator called each volunteer by phone to tell them of a fire..."

The responsibility of the early firefighters was extraordinary. The volunteers not only fought fires, but also planned fund-raising events to continually raise money to purchase new equipment. The members canvassed the neighborhoods for donations and held dances and pancake suppers. One of the longest running events was the annual Firemen's Carnival, held from 1926 to the mid-1950s. The early carnivals were exciting one- or two-day events. Carnival goers could purchase meals, observe fire department demonstrations and watch tournaments. In 1928 Farquhar wrote to The Maryland News, a county newspaper, to announce the carnival:

"The supper will be served on Wednesday Sept. 5th, with fried chicken, ham and other good things to make up a bountiful meal and it is expected this feature will attract many more than the 400 who were served last year. Special attention will be given to the evening attractions this year as city electric current will be available for the first time, and the grounds will be amply lighted."

Over the years the department expanded activities at the carnival. Parades, games and country-music shows were added. Each year the department raised between $1,300 to $2,000 and the carnival was a highlight of Sandy Spring summers.

The Annals for 1930-31 provides a flavor for the annual benefit, noting that "the season's thunderstorm came the afternoon of the Firemen's Carnival -- in time to stop the baseball game and the anticipated aerial display of Dalton Ervin. The Old Timers did their Horse Shoe pitching just the same. The excellent supper, the dancing and other features cleared $1,300.00 for the Department."

The Annals also noted that the ladies of the neighborhood found an outlet in planning the Firemen' card parties. The women worked out a complicated system of inviting friends, who in turn invited other lady friends. Each lady who attended a card party contributed 50 cents, thereby collecting as much money as possible to benefit the firehouse from their parties.

In 1930 the department built a permanent station at the corner of Route 108 and Meeting House Road. The cornerstone laying ceremony was interrupted by the sound of a fire alarm. Volunteers climbed aboard the engine and raced to a farm where a tenant house was burning. Fortunately the farmer and his men had extinguished the blaze by the time the firefighters arrived. Following the interruption, the firemen returned and the ceremony continued. In case help was needed to fight a fire, on-duty firefighters used a system to let off-duty volunteers know where a fire was raging. Initially they used a bell and later sounded a siren. The length and number of blasts of the siren indicated the direction of the fire.

Increased calls for first aid, ambulance services and rescue operations came with the growth of the Olney and Sandy Spring communities of the 1950s and 1960s. In 1962 the department hired two career firefighters to work the daytime shift. By the late 1960s the volunteers knew one station in Sandy Spring was not enough.

In 1971 the department's second station was opened on Georgia Avenue in Olney.

Today the department has a combination career/volunteer system that depends upon county tax dollars as well as contributions. The majority of calls involve accidents and rescue operations. New methods of home and commercial building construction and the department's aggressive fire prevention program resulted in a decrease in the number of fires in the area. One prevention program features Max, a Dalmation, who performs tricks to demonstrate fire safety techniques to thousands of area school children.

SANDY SPRING MUSEUM

The village of Sandy Spring grew up near a bubbling spring that was surrounded by white sand. The early settlers in the 1700s were members of the Religious Society of Friends, more commonly known as Quakers. As the community grew, they built their place of worship called a meeting house on land given by one of the Quaker families in the vicinity of the spring.

Those early settlers and succeeding generations of their families had a powerful influence on farming, education, business and community life that went far beyond the physical boundaries of the village. In the 1800s the Quakers from surrounding villages like Olney and Ashton referred to themselves as Sandy Springers. Sandy Spring became known as a "state of mind," not a place.

The Sandy Spring Museum was founded in 1980 to serve the communities within a six-mile radius of the Friends Meeting House on Meeting House Road. Olney, located three miles west of Sandy Spring, has always housed the museum.

The organization was begun by Delmas Wood. An insurance agent and auctioneer, Wood recognized that many valuable artifacts were sold to residents who lived outside the local communities. Wood's interest in a museum originated in the late 1970s when he arranged an auction of 500 oil paintings from the

Milton Bancroft estate on Norwood Road. Wood didn't know that Bancroft (1866-1947) was a well-respected artist and teacher, and he placed low prices on the paintings. Residents of the Washington Metropolitan area who knew Bancroft's work flocked to the auction and picked up the artwork at a bargain.

Afterwards Wood went to the Smithsonian Institution in Washington, D.C., to gather information about starting a museum. He enlisted the support of the Sandy Spring National Bank that made the first contribution, a check for $500. The bank also provided space for the museum's original collection in the basement of its Olney branch building. The building was torn down in 1987.

In 1985 museum members bought Tall Timbers, the home of the late Dr. Charles and Gladys Brooke Tumbleson on the Olney-Sandy Spring Road in Olney. Volunteers banded together to renovate the house. While working in the attic, volunteers discovered a hive of honey bees and called an exterminator. Later when the weather was hot, someone touched what appeared to be cracks in the walls of the house and discovered that the cracks were actually honey.

The Sandy Spring Museum, which officially opened at the Tall Timbers site in October 1986, has become an outstanding resource for the community. The museum acquires and collects artifacts. Staff and volunteers arrange exhibits and present programs on the history and customs of the surrounding communities. Many of the artifacts reflect the agricultural heritage of the area while others interpret and depict daily life of residents of the 18th, 19th and 20th centuries.

A living history project guarantees that residents of the 1990s will also have a place in local history. Bricks, engraved with individual or family names, pave the path through the fragrant herb garden on the west side of the museum. A biographical sketch of each name imprinted on a brick is filed at the museum. To insure that the museum will always remain in the community, the trustees have created an endowment fund at the Sandy Spring National Bank. Interest from the fund supports the museum's operation. An annual strawberry festival and other events are held to raise money to further the goals of the museum.

Chapter 10

BIRTH OF NEW OLNEY

The seeds of Olney's growth as a modern-day community were planted in the 1960s by the same land speculation that sparked the early birth of the village in the 1700s. Since those seeds were planted, the wave of growth has continued into the 1990s.

The first planned community in Olney was built in the early 1950s by Don Lamborne who lived at the historic Fair Hill homestead for a time. Lamborne selected colonial-style characteristics as the theme of his Williamsburg Village development.

Other builders recognized the potential for development in Olney, especially in the northwest quadrant of the intersection. They saw the rolling farmlands surrounding the town's intersection and envisioned a sea of houses instead of waving rows of grain. However county officials in the 1950s wanted to keep the Olney area rural to preserve the purity of the water supply in the Triadelphia and Rocky Gorge reservoirs that were located north and east of Olney.

PHOTO 18 The Olney intersection, looking south on Georgia Avenue. Photo courtesy of Mary Lane Schwartz.

The developers pushed county officials for an extension of public water and sewer. Although county civic groups resisted, the developers eventually won, and water and sewer services were extended to the Olney area. The village of Olney that had slowly grown to 2,500 people by 1965 was on the brink of change. Olney Mill, a community of about 900 homes, became the first development under the revised sewer and water policy. Other neighborhoods quickly sprouted.

Olney's explosive growth from the late 1960s to the present, has made it a modern-day community when compared with Brookeville to the north and Laytonsville to the west. Although farmers no longer export their produce and milk to Washington, newcomers have forged their own ties with the nation's capital. Residents work for the federal government or for private firms that have federal contracts. People also take advantage of entertainment in Washington -- museums, libraries, theaters -- and often spend the fourth of July and other holiday celebrations at free concerts, picnics, parades and political marches.

Newcomers have fought to keep the rural entryway to the community intact. Trees and grassy areas along Georgia Avenue, beginning at the Route 28 intersection, have been preserved to provide a buffer to the town and separate Olney from the string of commercial growth surrounding Aspen Hill and Wheaton.

Residents promote events held within the town. Banners strung between poles on the northeast corner of the Olney intersection announce upcoming events of the numerous nonprofit organizations that are the foundation of the community. Since the early 1980s groups have sponsored activities such as a town parade and a free military concert. Volunteers from these groups spend hours planning community events to raise money to operate their organizations. The local newspaper spotlights community news and monitors county government actions that affect the town. Olney residents have earned a reputation for "doing their homework" when asked to testify on town issues at county council and county planning board meetings.

THE GREATER OLNEY CIVIC ASSOCIATION

A glance at the trees, gazebo and grassy section at the Olney intersection provides a quick introduction to one project of the Greater Olney Civic Association. Commonly referred to as GOCA, the organization consists of representatives from the homeowners' associations in the area. GOCA holds monthly public meetings and invites residents to discuss community concerns during the public comments session that begins each meeting. GOCA is one of two organizations responsible for monitoring Olney's growth and promoting its sense of community. Often developers present their plans at GOCA meetings and seek favorable comment that they use to win county approval of their projects.

GOCA officers and members testify at county government hearings on Olney-related issues such as roads, schools, police and fire services. GOCA officers also lobby county council members and state legislators for the funding of local projects, especially when improvements are needed for roads and schools.

The precursor of GOCA, the Olney Citizens Association, was founded by Don Lamborne, the developer of Williamsburg Village. Lamborne formed the association in 1952 when postal officials tried to close the Olney Post Office. The group generated enough public pressure to keep the post office open.

In 1954 when Olney Elementary School was built on Georgia Avenue, civic group leaders and the new school's Parent Teacher Association invited Maryland Governor Theodore McKeldin as the keynote speaker at the school dedication. They took McKeldin and his wife to dinner at the Olney Inn. Then the McKeldins rode in Lamborne's 18th century horse-drawn coach to the school for the dedication ceremony.

The citizen's association was also instrumental in persuading Giant Food Corporation to build a colonial-style building in keeping with the colonial charm of the community, instead of a traditional-style grocery store. As more neighborhoods developed, the civic association expanded and eventually changed its name to the Greater Olney Civic Association. In 1978 the organization incorporated and initiated an awards ceremony to honor local residents who have made outstanding contributions to the community. Because of GOCA's reputation as a community "watch dog," county and state elected officials attend the annual awards ceremony, especially during election years.

Several of GOCA's achievements have become part of the fabric of the community and occasionally serve as a model for other communities. In the mid-1970s the U.S. Postal Service selected a new post office site without consulting the community. GOCA protested saying community representatives would have had better ideas for selecting convenient site locations than an outside agency. That complaint initiated a 1974 Congressional bill that called for greater community input in selecting sites for postal facilities.

In another situation GOCA and other residents grew tired of waiting for a promised library that seemed to disappear from the county budget each year. GOCA was successful in circulating a petition that persuaded county officials to move the construction of the library three years ahead of schedule. The one-story building with an attractive cathedral ceiling opened to the community in 1982.

Because of GOCA's efforts residents enjoy many other community benefits. The dream for Longwood Recreation Center became a reality after GOCA lobbied county government officials. During the mid-1980s the widening of Georgia Avenue from Route 28 to the Olney business district was mired in delay. GOCA suggested that the county government loan money to the state to begin construction to get the widening project underway. Since then the county used the same process to begin other state road projects.

Aside from working on development and legislative issues, GOCA has sponsored many community-wide events such as the

Olney Days Festival that was held in the early 1980s. Since 1989 GOCA has sponsored the Olney Parade which draws several thousand spectators. In the spring GOCA holds the Taste Of Olney, a fund-raising event that features food samples from area restaurants. The money goes to various GOCA projects such as the beautification of the Georgia Avenue/Route 108 intersection.

THE OLNEY CHAMBER OF COMMERCE

In the early 1960s, the Postal Service again threatened to close the Olney Post Office. This time the business community banded together to preserve Olney's identity.

The postal service had reviewed Olney's mail volume and decided it was insufficient to maintain a post office. The U.S. Postal Service wanted to move Olney's postal services to its Rockville site. But business leaders knew something the postal service didn't -- the community was growing and at that very moment, developers were drawing up plans to build houses on the surrounding farmland.

Business leaders realized that an organized effort offered the best chance to save Olney's post office. The Olney Chamber of Commerce was founded in 1964, and members lobbied congressional representatives. Their efforts paid off, and the U.S. Postal Service dropped the plans to move the community's postal service. The chamber also spoke out on zoning issues facing their small rural community and provided input into the 1966 Olney Master Plan. Initially the chamber had 22 charter members. In 1979 the chamber initiated a show-and-tell session so residents could learn about each business. Neighbors and friends came to listen, and the informal sessions often lasted well past midnight. The sessions became so popular that in 1982 the chamber switched to a trade show format, and businesses were provided with space to promote their services. Today over 3,000 people attend the free event, Community Night, which is held each October.

The chamber grew with the community, and today the group has over 200 members. Monthly dinner meetings are held during the school year. Members are active in the community, working with the county police department to keep commercial crime at a minimum and lobbying legislators to upgrade local roads. The chamber has also sponsored dances for Olney teenagers and has awarded college scholarships to local students each year.

THE OLNEY POST OFFICE

A look at the Olney Post Office of the 1960s shows why the U.S. Postal Service may have wanted to close it. The postmaster operated out of a corner of Armstrong Feed Store on the northeast side of Route 108. One postman delivered the mail -- to Brookeville homes in the morning and Olney homes in the afternoon. During the Christmas season, packages were stored in the postmaster's pickup truck because there was no room in the post office. During the '60s, folks in Olney came to the feed store to pick up mail, sit in front of the pot-bellied stove and trade stories.

When the Olney Mill community was developed in the late 1960s, mail volume increased. The Olney Chamber of Commerce, which had fought so hard to save the postal facility, felt vindicated. The community was delighted when the postal service took over the feed store and renovated it. But the story of Olney's post office didn't end with a renovated building. Since the former feed store was slated to be torn down for the intersection widening, the postal service bought a small parcel of farmland on Route 108, west of the intersection.

A new post office opened in 1975. At the time the postal facility seemed isolated from the rest of Olney. Corn fields surrounded the building, and the farmer who rented the land often dropped bags of corn at the post office for employees to enjoy. Today the fields are gone -- rows of townhouses replace the rows of corn. Numerous carriers deliver the Olney mail, and residents often stand in line to buy stamps or mail packages. As one retired postal clerk commented, "We still try to be friendly, but we don't have time to chat with everyone now."

THE OLNEY COURIER-GAZETTE

As a young man fresh out of college, Lon Anderson saw Olney as a perfect place for a newspaper -- the town had a growing business and residential community, and the civic association and chamber of commerce supplied a semi-official town voice.

Anderson and a friend bought the weekly Damascus Courier in 1972, changed the name to County Courier and extended coverage to Olney. Anderson described local events and the people behind the events. The weekly newspaper had a broadsheet format. Since the operation was fairly small, Anderson used Olney residents as columnists to chronicle everyday happenings.

Early newspaper stories described an evening of light-hearted dancing at the Olney Inn and reported a fire that destroyed the 70-year old Soper's Store. The newspaper gave accounts of citizens' complaints and suggestions on state plans for a widened Georgia Avenue/Route 108 intersection.

In the late 1970s Anderson sold his newspaper to the Providence Rhode Island Journal. Davis Kennedy, publisher of the Gaithersburg Gazette, bought controlling interest in 1982 and changed the name of the Olney paper to the Olney Courier-Gazette. The paper switched to a tabloid format.

The Gazette chain expanded and now includes 13 newspapers, each focusing on the community it serves. Coverage in the Olney paper encompasses Brookeville, Sandy Spring, Ashton, Brinklow and Unity-Sunshine. In 1992 The Washington Post Company bought 80 percent interest in the Gazette chain. A year later the Post Company purchased the remaining shares. However, the Gazette chain continues to be an independent weekly that has no relationship with The Washington Post newspaper.

FROM A SAVINGS INSTITUTION TO
THE SANDY SPRING NATIONAL BANK

The bank may have its headquarters in Olney but its history is buried deep in the soil of Sandy Spring.

Following the Civil War, the county, like most of the country, struggled to get back on its feet. Gold and silver prices had escalated, and borrowing money was difficult. In such an economy Sandy Spring seemed a most unlikely place to launch the county's first savings institution -- a farming community that boasted only one business, the Montgomery Mutual Fire Insurance Company. But the Quaker farmers wanted a place where they could save as well as borrow money.

Members of the Quaker community talked about their needs and on March 30, 1868, acquired a charter from the state. Each director contributed $3.50 to buy the accounting books and supplies, and the insurance company contributed space for the fledgling savings institution. On the first day of business, April 13, 1868, 44 people deposited $383.

According to bank history, the original directors could best be described as "frugal farmers." Since most were Quakers, "thrift was uppermost in their minds and saving came ahead of spending as the proper use of whatever income was left beyond the needs of a conservative mode of living."

Initially the savings institution, which was classified as a mutual savings bank, opened every Monday afternoon from 3-6 p.m. Later the bank expanded its hours and operated two days a week from 2-4 p.m. The majority of deposits went back into the community as home loans to area residents.

For the first few years the savings institution operated out of an existing room at the insurance office. By 1878 Montgomery Mutual spent $450 to add a room especially for the savings institution, and yearly rent totaled $25. In 1895 the institution had a building constructed beside the insurance company in Sandy Spring.

By 1900 customers wanted more options than the savings institution provided, like checking accounts. In addition, farmers wanted loans for those lean months while they waited for their harvest. Directors of the savings institution together with other community members decided they needed a bank. They raised $25,000 in capital and received a charter for the First National Bank of Sandy Spring. Both the bank and savings institution operated in the same building and often had the same president and occasionally the same employees. Some directors served on both boards.

In 1920 a robbery and murder at the bank/savings institution made the front page of newspapers in the state and resulted in the founding of the Maryland State Police. Five men with guns walked into the bank one spring afternoon and told the six employees to raise their hands. Frank Hallowell, an employee, was deaf and did not understand the instructions. He was shot and killed. The rest of the employees were locked in the vault and the robbers escaped with more than $36,000.

The county sheriff and his deputies could not catch the robbers, and the more experienced detectives from Baltimore could not reach the scene quickly enough to help. The suspects were eventually caught, but the robbery and killing highlighted the need for a state police force, which was founded soon after.

Both financial institutions came to Olney in 1956, renting space in a two-story cinder-block building in the northeast quadrant of the intersection. Together in 1963 they financed the construction of a colonial style office building in the southeast quadrant, but the building no longer stands.

Many residents considered the two separate entities, the savings institution and the bank, as "The Sandy Spring Bank." By 1972 the two boards finally agreed it was time to join together, giving birth to the Sandy Spring National Bank and Savings Institution.

As the institution grew and opened more branches, larger quarters were needed. The bank, which had already purchased the old Olney Inn property, decided to build its new headquarters on the site. The new colonial-style building opened in the fall of 1986.

OTHER BUSINESSES

The 1980 Olney Master Plan, prepared by the county planning board, envisioned a community of homes, townhouses, apartments and condominiums served by convenience-type stores rather than large department stores or malls. The plan was successful.

The three shopping centers that developed between 1970 and 1990 feature dry cleaning establishments, a drug store, grocery stores, flower, book and card shops, sports equipment, a pet shop and specialty clothing stores. Several restaurants line the business district. Olney has also attracted doctors, dentists, accountants and computer specialists.

SCHOOLS

Nothing pulls the community together faster than a controversy involving the schools. In 1981 the superintendent of schools announced that Olney Elementary School would be closed because there would not be enough students. The community, led by GOCA, made door-to-door surveys, collected statistics on the current residents and estimated population increases for the next few years. Armed with statistics and petitions, Olney residents persuaded school officials to keep Olney Elementary open. Less than 10 years later the school was overcrowded, and again citizens battled the government for expansion and modernization that was completed in 1991.

Olney's growth pattern can be seen in the development of its schools. Olney Elementary School was built in 1954 to relieve overcrowding at Sherwood Elementary School then located on the Sherwood High School campus in Sandy Spring. In 1967 a new building was constructed for Sherwood Elementary several miles west of the high school campus.

William H. Farquhar Middle School was built in 1968 and was the first county school to serve sixth, seventh and eighth graders exclusively. It seems appropriate that the school was named after the first president of the school board, a Sandy Spring Quaker. The early growth of Olney in the late 1960s and early 1970s led to the construction of other schools. Greenwood Elementary was built in 1970, and Belmont Elementary was constructed in 1974. Brooke Grove Elementary was built in 1990, a year earlier than expected. The new building served as a holding school for Olney Elementary students while the 1954 building was renovated. Brooke Grove opened as a school in 1991 to relieve overcrowding at Olney Elementary and to serve the new developments in the northeast quadrant of Olney.

Rosa Parks, a new middle school, was opened in 1992. A future elementary school is planned for a proposed neighborhood on the southwest edge of Olney.

FUTURE

According to the 1980 Master Plan, Olney is almost built out. Since so much of Olney is new in comparison to historic Brookeville and Laytonsville, it is difficult to find remnants of old Olney. But history can be found in unexpected places -- the former Rockland School for Girls, now a private residence; the Olney House, a commercial building on Route 108 just east of the intersection; Longwood, a house built in the early 1800s for Thomas Moore; St. John's Episcopal Church founded in 1842 and Finneyfrocks Shop with its display of tools of the 19th century blacksmith trade. But the greatest lifeline to the past of this former farming community is the Sandy Spring Museum.

The new Olney has much to offer -- new traditions, modern-day conveniences and a proud history. Residents, both oldtimers and newcomers, are strongly committed to protecting the small-town community life they love. Echoes of Olney's past remain for those who are eager to explore the heritage of Olney.

140

Bibliography

Annals of Sandy Spring. 4 vols, 1883-1947. Sandy Spring, Md.: Privately printed.

Autobiography of Benjamin Hallowell. Second edition. Philadelphia: Friends' Book Association, 1884.

Boyd, T.H.S. *The History of Montgomery County, Maryland*. 1879. Reprint. Baltimore, Md.: Clearfield Comp., 1989.

Calendar of Maryland State Papers, Number 4, Part 2, The Red Books. Maryland: The Hall of Records Commission No. 8.

Farquhar, Roger Brooke. *Old Homes and History of Montgomery County, Md*. 1962. Reprint. Brookeville Md.: American History Research Associates, 1981.

Farquhar, William Henry. *Annals of Sandy Spring*. 1884. Reprint. Cottonport, La.: Polyanthos, Inc., 1971.

Hiebert, Ray Eldon, and Richard K. MacMaster. *A Grateful Remembrance: the Story of Montgomery County, Maryland*. Rockville, Md.: The Montgomery County Government and the Montgomery County Historical Society, 1976.

Hopkins, G.M., comp. *Atlas of Fifteen Miles Around Washington including The County of Montgomery Maryland*. 1879. Reprint. Rockville, Md.: Montgomery County Historical Society, 1975.

Ickes, Harold L. *The Secret Diary of Harold Ickes*. 3 vols. New York: Simon and Schuster, 1953-54.

Jacobs, Charles T. *Civil War Guide To Montgomery County, Maryland*. Rockville, Md.: The Montgomery County Historical Society and the Montgomery County Civil War Round Table, 1983.

Jenkins, Mary, and Eben Jenkins. *The First Hundred Years, Maryland State Grange 1874-1974*. Silver Spring, Md.: Maryland State Grange, 1974.

Jewell, E. Guy. *From One Room to Open Space: A History of Montgomery County Public Schools from 1732 to 1965.* Rockville, Md.: Montgomery County Public Schools, 1976.

Land, Aubrey C. "A Land Speculator in the Opening of Western Maryland." *Maryland Historical Magazine* 1953.

Lea, Elizabeth Ellicott. *Domestic Cookery, Useful Receipts, and Hints to Young Housekeepers.* In *A Quaker Woman's Cookbook,* edited with an Introduction by William Woys Weaver. Philadelphia, Pa.: University of Pennsylvania Press, 1982.

Nesbitt, Martha C., and Mary Reading Miller. *Chronicles of Sandy Spring Friends Meeting and Environs.* Sandy Spring, Md.: Sandy Spring Monthly Meeting of the Religious Society of Friends, 1987.

One Hundred Years of Savings in Sandy Spring 1868-1968. Sandy Spring, Md.: Sandy Spring National Bank, 1968.

Scharf, J. Thomas. *History of Western Maryland.* Vol. 1. 1882. Reprint. Baltimore, Md.: Regional Publishing Co., 1968.

Stabler, Harold B. *Some Further Recollections.* Sandy Spring, Md.: Privately printed, 1963.

Sween, Jane C. *Montgomery County: Two Centuries of Change.* Woodland Hills, Ca.: Windsor Publications, Inc., 1984.

Watkins, T.H. *Righteous Pilgrim, The Life and Times of Harold Ickes, 1874-1952.* New York: Henry Holt, 1990.